WOODSTOCK
FESTIVAL REMEMBERED

WOODSTOCK
FESTIVAL REMEMBERED

by Jean Young and Michael Lang

BALLANTINE BOOKS • NEW YORK

To Ann Lang, Artie and
Linda Kornfeld, and Peter Goodrich
—M.L.

To Jim Young for all his help and
Michael Young for his encouragement
—J.Y.

Acknowledgment

The authors would like to express their appreciation to those in
the Woodstock Community who have helped in the preparation
of this book, especially Allan Gordon, Bob Reynolds, Michael
Green, and Tisha Bernuth. A very special thanks is also due
Henry Diltz for his contribution.

Book designed by Constance Timm

Photographs by Henry Diltz: Copyright © 1969 by Henry Diltz
Photographs by Gerald Hochman: Copyright © 1969 by Gerald Hochman
Photographs by Elliott Landy: Copyright © 1969 by Elliott Landy
Photographs by Barry Z Levine: Copyright © 1969 by Barry Z Levine
Photographs by Lee Marshall: Copyright © 1978 by Lee Marshall

Cover photographers—Henry Diltz, Elliott Landy, Lee Marshall

BLACK AND WHITE PHOTO CREDITS:

Henry Diltz pp. 6, 7, 8, 9, 10, 11, 12, 13, 14, 15, 16, 17, 18, 19, 20, 21, 22, 23, 24, 25, 26,
27, 28, 29, 30, 31, 97, 98, 99, 100, 101, 102, 103, 107, 108, 109, 110, 111, 112, 113,114,
115, 116, 117, 118, 119, 120, 121, 122, 123, 124, 125, 126, 127; Elliott Landy p. 122; Barry
Z Levine p. 8; Lee Marshall pp. 20, 32, 104, 105, 106, 107, 120, 121, 123.

COLOR PHOTO CREDITS:

Henry Diltz pp. 34, 35, 36, 37, 38, 39, 40, 41, 44, 45, 48, 49, 51, 52, 53, 54,55, 58, 59, 60, 62,
63, 64, 65, 66, 67, 70, 76, 77, 80, 81, 82, 83, 84, 85, 86, 87, 88, 89, 90, 91, 92, 93, 94, 95;
Gerald Hochman pp. 54, 61, 70, 71; Elliott Landy pp. 50, 51, 58, 59, 60, 61, 62, 64, 65,
68, 69, 72, 73, 74, 75, 76, 78, 79, 83, 86, 88, 89, 93, 96; Barry Z Levine pp. 38, 42, 44, 46,
47, 49, 56, 57, 66, 70, 71, 76, 77, 90, 91; Lee Marshall pp. 42, 43, 44, 45, 47, 48, 50, 51,
58, 60, 86; p. 33 Copyright © 1969 Woodstock Ventures, Ltd.

Library of Congress Cataloging in Publication Data

Young, Jean.
    Woodstock Festival Remembered.

    1. Woodstock Festival I. Lang, Michael, joint author. II. Title.
ML38.W66Y7   784   78-71169
ISBN 0-345-28003-2

Manufactured in the United States of America

First Edition: 1979

1   2   3   4   5   6   7   8   9

PREFACE

In August 1969, two million people attempted to get to a 660-acre dairy farm in White Lake, New York, about 100 miles north of New York City, to listen to rock music, camp out, and just be together. Five hundred thousand people got there. The word they used then was "groove." They came from all over the United States for the Woodstock Aquarian Music and Art Fair (better known as the Woodstock Festival), which was to have a powerful impact on world youth culture and on the way many young people today look at and live in the world.

It has been said that Woodstock was the largest peacetime gathering in history. It was remarkable not only for its size but for the peacefulness and joy of the event, which set it apart from other rock festivals of the time, such as that in Altamont, California, where violence prevailed. The Woodstock Festival showed the world that hundreds of thousands of youths could join together in peace, endure three days of rain and mud, share music, pleasure, and hardship, and live together virtually without violent confrontation. The chief physician at the festival reported that there were no injuries as a result of violent incidents.

This book reflects a special time and celebrates the young people and performers of the late Sixties who came to be known as the "Woodstock Generation." It is a record of a time, a place, and a people—the youth of 1969, the end of an age of innocence, before the shootings at Kent State and Jackson State quashed the student protest movement, demoralized the antiwar movement, and led toward the depressing revelations of Watergate. We—and they—are ten years older now, but Woodstock has left an indelible mark on our country. Newspapers and television and the film *Woodstock* spread a vision of youth which helped to liberalize drug and abortion laws and led to more relaxed dress codes in schools, offices, and on the street. The Woodstock Festival synergized a way of life which had been growing through the Sixties: antiwar, antiestablishment, pro-drugs, noncompetitive, and individualistic. Rock music was the anthem for all this social change, and its sound and lyrics said, in the words of Bob Dylan, "the times they are a'changin'."

The press was often arch, skeptical, and condescending in its coverage of the Woodstock Festival. YOUNG PEOPLE DIE OF DOPE . . . YOUNG PEOPLE EXPERIENCE REDUCTION TO STARK ANIMAL STATUS. These headlines might have sold newspapers, but they didn't describe what really happened at Woodstock. This book does, from the vantage point of Michael Lang, the man who conceived and planned it. It also reflects the memories of many others who were *there*, in the mud, in the crowd, sharing food, swapping, buying, selling, smoking the free grass, and listening to the free music. Yes, for most of the multitude, the music was free. The people who bought their tickets in advance were the only ones who paid. There were no ticket booths at the Woodstock Festival.

There were dancing day and night, lovemaking and nude bathing, and the feeling of being free with hundreds of thousands of friends. There is a visual feast in store for you here—hundreds of photographs of the festival, showing the way it really was. Once again, it is August 15, 16, and 17, 1969, and you are at the Woodstock Aquarian Music and Art Fair. You may never see its like again.

WOODSTOCK:
Putting It Together

To recall in detail the events that took place during the planning and execution of the Woodstock Festival would fill many volumes. I shall leave that task to someone else and instead try to give the reader a feeling of what the experience was like for me as I lived through those events.

I was in Miami at the beginning of the Sixties movement, which started in the Haight-Ashbury section of San Francisco and the East Village in New York's Lower East Side. I opened a head shop in the Cocoanut Grove section of Miami, which was a kind of a center for the "underground," selling papers, posters, pipes, and all kinds of head stuff. I was not into doing shows or concerts at all; in fact, I knew nothing about the music business at the time.

The festival concept grew out of those times. With me, it started in Miami about the time it was starting everywhere else. We were looking for another way to relate to people, not the usual competitive, restrained, or prejudiced relationship. The festival was part of an alternative lifestyle, like the commune, and reflected the idea of people living together and helping one another out.

In Miami I started a partnership with three guys to produce concerts. One of them was Rick O'Feldman, a dolphin trainer at the time, Barry Toran, who was my attorney, and a drummer by the name of James Baron. We decided to do concerts, and live music came south with acts like Ravi Shankar, Steppenwolf, and the Grateful Dead. Somewhere along the line we decided it would be a great idea to do a festival. We looked around for a place and decided on Gulf Stream Park, a racetrack in Miami. There had been very few concerts of any kind in Florida, and at first the management didn't know what we were proposing. We finally got them to agree to rent us the track. The festival was going to be backed partially by ourselves and partially by a man named Marshall Brevitz. Unfortunately, Marshall had certain conditions tied to his money: We had to do the show within two weeks. I called Hector Moralles, who was a booking agent at the William Morris office in New York, and asked him to help me book the acts we needed. He told me I was crazy to try to put on a show of that size in only two weeks, but, as I said, due to the financial pressure I really had no choice. Confirmation of the acts came only three days before the show, so we only had three days in which to advertise it. We managed to book Jimi Hendrix, The Mothers of Invention, The Blues Image, Blue Cheer, John Lee Hooker, Chuck Berry, and Arthur Brown. We figured it would be an outrageous show and would open up what was at the time a tight Top 40 music scene.

We needed a stage and a PA system, and with the help of Stanley Goldstein, a recording engineer, we raided Criteria Studios and took all of their PA

HENRY DILTZ

Michael Lang and Tisha Bernuth

Artie Kornfeld

Peter Goodrich

equipment. In thinking back, Mac Immerman, who owned Criteria, must have had a lot of guts to let all that equipment out of his studio. We couldn't figure out how to build stages quickly that would hold everybody securely. We called around and found six flatbed trucks and rolled them onto the track. We set them up two by two so that we could structure the show on three rotating stages. It was going to be a two-day event, two shows a day, afternoon and evening. We rented out booths to sell head-shop gear and assorted psychedelia.

We managed to get everything arranged and the crowds came. After the music began we realized somebody had forgotten to pick up Hendrix at the airport. I sent cars out to get him, but Jimi had gotten impatient and decided to rent a helicopter. This turned out to be beautiful. Just as Jimi was due to go on stage and we were going berserk, this helicopter came hovering over the stage and Jimi comes down a ladder. He played an incredible set. I guess the seed for Woodstock was sown during the Miami Pop Festival.

I was up on the scaffolding watching the evening show and looked down at the audience, which was a pretty straight-looking crowd. There weren't too many long-hairs in the South back then, and everybody was just sitting there with totally engrossed looks on their faces, just staring at the stage in amazement. It was a nice feeling, everybody just sort of digging on the music. I couldn't believe it was working that well.

It wasn't. The second day we almost got rained out. We had been in the middle of a drought, so we hadn't bothered to get rain insurance. Sunday morning the city decided to seed the clouds. No one could go on stage because they were afraid of being electrocuted, but Arthur Brown was there and he was insisting, "Please let me go on. It would be beautiful." We didn't think the sight of Arthur frying would be beautiful. I said no. And this guy from the crowd got up on stage and tried to start a riot because nobody was playing. We had to think of how to cool everyone out, so I went into the money room, where there was a big argument going on, and took $750. I ran out and slapped it into John Lee Hooker's hand because he had an acoustic guitar and wouldn't get electrocuted. He got right up there on stage and did a number—a talking blues about what was going on at the show. It should have been an album, because it was a great piece. He sang for about an hour and mellowed everyone out. In spite of all the hassles that weekend, Gulf Stream had less trouble than they had ever had at any of their normal race weekends. Everyone was pleased.

Shortly after the Miami Pop Festival I moved to Woodstock, New York, and rented a barn home. It was all very rustic. In New York I met Artie Kornfeld in a record-company office where I was trying to get a contract for a group I was managing called The Train. Artie was a successful writer and producer and was vice-president of A & R and Capitol Records. We became close friends very quickly. Like me, he was from the Bensonhurst section of Brooklyn.

I was trying to put together a concert series in the Woodstock area, and one evening I was talking to Artie about it. I asked him what he thought about the idea of doing a festival. He got very excited. That's how the idea actually got moving—talking with Artie. The time was ripe for it, and Woodstock was a better place than the track in Florida had been. I also wanted to do a recording studio in the country because there was so much talent around Woodstock. The Band was just starting to happen, Bob Dylan was there, Janis Joplin was around, and the town itself had a history of art, music, and crafts.

Artie and I took the idea to my lawyer, Miles Lourie, and he said he knew a couple of guys who were building a recording studio called Media Sound and they might go for the festival idea. I don't know where the story came from that I met John Roberts and Joel Rosenman by answering their ad in the paper: "Young men with unlimited capital looking for interesting, legitimate investment opportunities and business propositions." They claim they did run the ad, but I have never seen it.

Artie and I went to Joel's and John's apartment in Manhattan. It was like a big smile and a big handshake and the whole thing. They were really straight kids—two young executives on their way up. That was the impression they gave. I wasn't really ready for them, and they didn't know what to make of me at all, so I didn't say very much. Artie got along with them really well and so he took over. I sort of watched and listened. They thought it was a nice idea, this thing about music and art in the country with streams and pastures. I guess it's the kind of picture we created. We also talked about our studio idea, tying it in. They got very excited about the whole thing. Every once in a while I'd look up and see this very strange "What is it?" look on their faces.

Mel Lawrence

Michael Wadleigh

Steve Cohen and John Morris

Somehow they seemed really hungry to find out what it was all about, like, why do you seem so happy? At the time they had never heard of Hermann Hesse or Jimi Hendrix. But I was sure that if they were willing to take a chance, the whole idea would grow on them.

We brought with us a simple two-page budget, which called for an initial investment of about $500,000. They reviewed it and seemed pleased. We went back to see them a couple of days later, but meanwhile we found some other people who were interested in backing the idea. We told Joel and John, "Listen, we found some people in the music business who want to put up the money for the festival, so we don't think we will be able to do it with you guys." Apparently they had decided to do it because Joel sat down looking crushed. "God damn it," he shouted, "every time we decide to do something, some big corporation comes in and takes it away from us." So we decided that we would do it with them. I guess we felt kind of sorry for them. We were all about the same age. John was the oldest, about twenty-four.

When Artie and I went to see Joel's and John's lawyer, Arnold Copelson, I kept my mouth shut and Artie took the ball again. He had a better rap. We spent three or four hours talking about the whole project and how everything was going to be put together. Copelson finally turned to me and said he understood pretty much what the project was about and about Artie's function, but what was I going to do? I said, "I know how to pull it off."

I have this belief in people. This is the reason I took a chance on Woodstock and undertook the responsibility. It was kind of an ultimatum to myself, so I had to make sure the whole thing was right on. I had this idea that the purpose of government was to protect your freedoms, not to protect you from yourself. Beyond that, it seemed to me that the purpose of power was kind of a jive. At the time we were coming out of a period where everyone was talking about how groovy everything was and quickly turning into a revolutionary kind of head, without ever giving "peace a chance." The chance I had in mind was Woodstock. I wanted to keep the political side of the movement at a distance and know whether the change from "flower power" to "revolutionary power" was coming out of the people or the environment. So for me Woodstock was conceived as a music-and-art fair.

But I'm getting ahead of myself. After making the deal with Joel and John, we got some offices and started planning. Stanley Goldstein and I drew up some organization charts and then began to search for people to fill the various roles: staging production, engineering, security, sanitation, crowd control, parking, etc., etc.

At first I tried to get Tom Driscoll and Tom Rounds, who had done the second Miami Pop Festival, to be the line producers for us. They were very together and had the experience we needed. They asked $50,000 apiece plus some points. I had offered them much less and they turned it down. They felt that it was an impossible thing to try and do. But being as determined as I was, I decided to go ahead without them and oversee the production myself. After the festival I got a wire from

Michael Goldstein, Mel Lawrence, and Michael Lang

11

Chip Monck

Peter Goodrich

Rounds and Driscoll saying we accept your offer. Mel Lawrence, who had come out with them to see me, decided to stay and came to work for us. Mel was head of the site operations—the whole physical thing—layout and landscaping.

From the start, Artie's job was publicity. Artie and I hired a concern called Wartoke to do public relations. Artie contributed a lot of energy getting the festival going. Joel, John, and Artie worked uptown, and I had a production office downtown in the Village. Artie made sure that the feeling was right on the logo design, publicity, and promotion that we put out.

Chris Langhart became our technical director and was a genius. He is an engineer and stage designer and also did the plumbing and electrical plans for us. He had taught theater design at New York University at the time, and he had helped put together the Fillmore East. For lighting I hired Chip Monck, who had done Monterey and was the best lighting man in the business at the time. Chip recommended John Morris to do artist relations, and the more people we put on staff, the more were recommended. Everyone knew people who were good at certain things. We found Joyce Mitchell, and she became the administrator of the downtown office. We then found Jim Mitchell, who was to become our purchasing agent. Peter Goodrich, an old friend of mine from Miami, was placed in charge of concessions, and I hired Tisha Bernuth to be my assistant. Together we found Wes Pomeroy, who was head of the President's Crime Commission, to be our head of security. Wes brought with him the Reverend Don Genung to be in charge of community relations and hired police chiefs from various places around the country to be his assistants.

Uptown, Artie and Joel had hired Keith O'Connor to head the ticketing operation and Bert Cohn and Michael Foreman, of Concert Hall, to do the advertising. They turned out to be ineffective, so Artie took over the area himself. The main contribution Bert and Mike made to the project, as I recall, was to design and install some unattractive and uncomfortable "groovy spaces" in the uptown facility.

Bill Hanley was our sound contractor. He was a major contractor for PAs and sound systems at the time. He did a great job for us, and I thought the sound was incredible in terms of its strength and its clarity. He recorded the entire show on two 8-track machines. Bill and Eddie Cramer had engineered and taped 40 hours of music. We contracted for Josh White's Light Show, and when the screen was not blowing over the stage it worked very well.

One of my responsibilities was to book the acts. One of the first things I did when I came to New York after the Miami festival was to spend about six months in Hector Moralles' office watching him work—six hours a day every day. Hector and I had become good friends after the Miami thing, and he schooled me on it all—the whole business of concert promotion: who books the acts, how you pay for the act, how they're booked. I wanted to take Woodstock to a place where festivals had never been before, but I had to start with the standard operations.

The first three acts we tried to book asked twice their normal fee from us, and Hector was outraged. I told him to go ahead and book them and give them the price they were asking. I knew that it would be hard for an "unknown" to book at all, and the Miami Pop wasn't enough to give me a place in the music world. I had to establish credibility, and the best way to do it was to get the ball rolling. The first three acts were the Jefferson Airplane, Canned Heat, and Credence Clearwater Revival—at $10,000 apiece. That may not seem like much these days, but at the time it was a lot of money for an act to earn for one show. When these three acts were committed we began to embellish Woodstock as a real event, the kind that everyone would just have to come to. I'm a great fan of using rumors as a promotional device. I went to Steven Paul's club in Manhattan, the Scene, one night and talked to a few people. I told them that there was going to be a gigantic festival at Woodstock that summer and described how I envisioned it. Two days later I got feedback from San Francisco and Los Angeles.

I wanted Bob Dylan there because he was responsible for a big part of the culture. I spent an hour at his Woodstock house and suggested that he come on in an unofficial way, knowing that he was sort of hiding out at the time. Dylan said, "I will stop by if I can." He never did, for he had made definite plans to attend and perform at the Isle of Wight Festival in England.

I tried to create a kind of democracy among the musicians by listing the acts in alphabetical order on

Steve Cohen

posters and advertising so there would be no top billing. In booking I didn't lean toward a black audience. The black performers we booked didn't play real black music; it was contemporary blues. It wasn't done consciously and I guess I'm sorry I didn't put in more blues. I wasn't thinking about the music in that context and maybe I should have. I was just working with the cultural background that was real to me. A lot of black people didn't listen to Jimi Hendrix's or Richie Havens' music. Ten to fifteen percent of the audience was black, but not ghetto blacks or blacks from the deep South. They were more the black people who had gotten into the whole Sixties movement. In booking, I just wanted to have enough types of music so that everyone would be covered. We tried to book Roy Rogers, for instance. The idea was to have Roy sing "Happy Trails" as the closing number for the festival. I thought it would have been a sweet touch. But his agent declined. I asked someone about Johnny Cash; he was undecided about whether or not to come. Finally he didn't, and it was too bad because he was the only Country Western performer we tried to book.

The downtown office was the production center. It was really a straight-ahead operation. Everything carried the feeling of what we were trying to do because I knew that the image you put out was the one you were going to get back. I guess that was why I had trouble letting anything get too far out of my control. The team of people we had worked really well together, but for a while I had the feeling that I was the only one who really knew where it was all leading. John Morris, for example, at one point, wanted to change the name of the festival and remove Woodstock from its title. He didn't feel that the name was important and thought it would hamper people in finding the site. They found it.

While the initial booking and staff preparations were going on, we were scouring the upstate area for a site. The one I found, with the help of Jimmy Young, a friend from Woodstock, was not working out. Joel and John, on their way back to New York City one day, came across an industrial site in the town of Wallkill. It was owned by a man by the name of Howard Mills. They called me and I went up with Mel and a few other people to check it out. It wasn't ideal, but Mel and Chip thought that we could make it work. I told Joel to go ahead and secure it, as time was going by rapidly. They made arrangements with Mills and thought that they had gotten a firm agreement with the town planning board. So we made arrangements for Mel and some members of the staff to move up and begin work on the site—landscaping, layout, and design. Meanwhile, the rest of the staff was back in New York working on designs and plans and figuring out how to deal with the huge task of building and operating a temporary city which would sustain the folks coming to the show. I was splitting my time between the office and the site trying to keep an overview on all the operations. Our community-relations man, the Reverend Don Genung, moved right in over a bar in the building which used to house the local brothel. Don was a very independent type and had his own peculiar way of doing things. I seem to remember Don being involved in a strange incident with the daughter of some local official, for example.

As I was nearing the completion of the bookings for the festival, John Morris, after spending a long night convincing The Who that it made sense for them to come from England to do the show, came into the office with a grim look on his face. "Bill Graham is going to pull this show out from under us," he said. I calmed him down, and he explained that we had booked many of the acts that Bill was planning to play at the Fillmore East that spring and summer. Bill could and would stop us to avoid the obvious dent we'd make in his business. I told John to set up a meeting for me with Bill, and the two of us would work it out. We met the next day at Ratner's, a restaurant next door to the Fillmore, and I proposed a solution. Concerning the acts scheduled to play both his shows and mine, I would advertise their names in mass media only after they had played his venue. He agreed and said, "We both can't play God on the same day" and offered to close the Fillmore East that weekend and come to the show.

Stanley Goldstein, our ambassador-at-large and head of campsites, was a big fan of the Hog Farmers, a communal group that lived out west. He loved the Hog Farmers with a passion. He wanted me to ask them to the festival. I met with Wavy Gravy, and he was kind of excited by the idea but had some doubt as to whether it would really come off at first. In any case, I said we would get back in touch with them. Several months later Stanley went out to see

HENRY DILTZ

David Potbelly

Wavy Gravy

their big bus race in New Mexico and again asked them to come and they agreed. We rented a plane for about 80 of them at a cost of $17,000, and they all came out. I understand on the way back the stewardesses locked themselves in the bathrooms, and the pilot asked the guitar player to come up front so they could hear the music. It must have been a wonderful trip, and I understand there's some great footage of it on film.

About that time Abbie Hoffman was coming around to my office in the Village wanting to talk to John or Joel. Abbie finally reached John by phone, and John felt threatened, so we decided to talk with him: Abbie was accusing us of ripping off the culture. We went down to his place in the East Village and met with him and several of the other movement people, people from the radical press and people from various East Village organizations. They were at their yippie best. It was kind of a game. We were outside while they were yipping around inside. John and Joel were in their suits and ties. We went in and it was very tense. We started talking. Abbie started demanding, give us this, give us that, and I said, "We're not going to give you anything. If you want to come and work with us, if you're really that concerned about the people who are going to be ripped off, that they're not going to have toilets, that they're not going to have medical care, that they're not going to have water and this and that, and that they won't know what to do with themselves in case of an emergency, why don't you put out a daily newsletter? We'll give you some money to build a booth and get a printing press." As it turned out, they did put out a newsletter, but most of the money went to the Chicago Eight trial.

Somewhere along the line things started to get weird between John, Joel, Artie, and me. There was a lot of insanity going on in the uptown office. I had gone out of town to check on a festival that was happening. There were riots at most of the larger shows and festivals that summer and spring, and I was trying to discover the real causes behind them. As it turned out, most of the problems were caused by unnecessary confrontations with police, usually decked out in riot gear, and by poor handling of gate-crashers. To avoid this problem, and to avoid any "bad vibes," we decided to provide free stages and free food and campsites to those coming to our show without tickets or money. We all knew that the festival could in no way come up to the expectations of everyone who was going to be a part of it; it had to inspire us all to be the things that we were looking for society to be. It had to go beyond the skepticism of its critics and the hustle of the movement and happen for real.

While I was gone things came to a head between Artie, John, and Joel. Joel and John did not want to sign Artie into the corporation, and I was holding his shares in my name at the time because for some reason he couldn't accept them until a certain date. We planned to bring him into the company April 15, but Joel and John decided that Artie wasn't putting it out. At the same time they were convinced that I was plotting to have a free festival. I guess I was pretty unimpressed with money at the time; I've changed my attitude since. It was simply that I felt it was something that I didn't need that much, but I certainly had nothing against it. It wasn't that I didn't want everyone to make money; I just wanted to get it on. I was leaving the financial maneuverings to Joel and John, and all of my time was taken up with getting the actual production together. They couldn't understand the mystery that existed between all of us, but regarding Artie, I was trying to keep up a wall so that the thing about his not coming into the corporation after it was agreed that he would, wouldn't explode. I felt I just had to keep the whole thing moving, but finally it became too much. Before going to the Atlanta Pop Festival I told Joel and John: "Work it out with Artie. But as far as I'm concerned, he's got his points." It was mad. Joel rushed to Artie's house and said, "Michael's done it. He's left. He's never coming back." When I got back I told Artie to talk to them about it, and I told John and Joel to talk to Artie about it, but I never could understand why they couldn't talk to each other about it.

John was always a man of his word, even though he really looked at the project as a comedy of errors. I don't think he ever had a grasp of what was involved in doing it. And Joel, too, not understanding it and not being around to see how it was really functioning, just had no grasp of what was happening. Joel and John were calling me all the time telling me we had to get rid of Artie, and I would say why do we have to get rid of Artie, and they'd say, "Because he's crazy." Artie would get excited about

Painting the mural for bridge

some idea that he had in his head, and they would go right out the window. They would say, "It's time for us to start a record company" or "It's time for us to start a publishing company." It wasn't like Artie was trying to rip them off—he was really into these things, and they weren't. He was into ideas, but they felt he wasn't taking care of the things that he was supposed to be taking care of. In spite of all the confusion and paranoia, Artie was signed into the company, and through it all John and Joel hung on and stayed with it. Things settled down a bit between us and we kept going.

Suddenly, after months of work on the Wallkill site, the town board claimed that they had never actually given permission for the festival and the events had been misinterpreted by John and Joel. We spent weeks trying to convince them to let us continue. About four weeks before the actual date of the festival the shocking reality came to me. They really could keep us out legally and, even if they couldn't, a lot of people were going to get hurt if we stayed. There was a lot of hostility there at the time.

There's a lot to the democratic process. I thought we were doing something that was very much in the spirit of America. I always had respect for the Founding Fathers and their concepts. I thought it was a good plan; maybe it got a little fouled up. Going through those processes and actually dealing with local politics and the corruption and how people finally will come through flashed on me at Wallkill. For instance, we went to that last meeting trying to convince the town board and the townspeople to give us the permits we needed, and I got up and talked about what we believed in—I just made a little speech. I felt the thing that everybody was really afraid of was their own children. I felt I had to break through all the rhetoric of the hippie image and get down to a real people-to-people communication. When it got down to that, communicating on a gut level, the hostile looks disappeared. It got down to where people really didn't know why they were against us. They were scared and confused by what we were proposing to do in their town, but they started to see us as people, not invading monsters to be feared and avoided. I felt we really reached them, but it didn't help at all in getting the permits. It did confirm in my mind, however, that if we could communicate to a right-wing community and really get through to them on that level, then we could get through to anybody.

As it happened, we had a call that same Friday from somebody in White Lake asking us to come up and see a site. When we got there, it turned out to be a swamp they wanted to have dredged out. Mel and I were riding around with a local real-estate agent and found Max Yasgur's farm. I saw this field that was perfect. It had a little rise at the bottom of this big bowl—a great site for a stage. It was a 40-acre natural bowl. Between Friday night and Saturday morning Max and I made a deal on the land. On Saturday afternoon we had the trucks loaded at Wallkill. By Saturday evening everything was moving on its way to White Lake. From that day we had fewer than four weeks to get ready, and only four of those days were without rain!

Max Yasgur was really something. He was straight,

upstanding, a backbone-of-America kind of guy. He had his prejudices, but he went beyond them. By the time we were close to being ready the whole town was on his back. Max was one of the wealthiest men in the community, and until the show was over he stood alone in that town. I feel that it was a privilege to have worked with him. Max had had a heart attack and he kept an oxygen tent in the bedroom in his house. It seemed that everytime I called and said I was coming over to give him some more bad news about what we'd done to the land that day, Max would be waiting in his oxygen tent to see me. He had made a deal with us and he was going to stick by it—he was totally honest. Any hint of corruption or payoff would drive him mad. He really made me feel as though I weren't in it alone.

The move from Wallkill had been expensive. All the preparations had been a total loss, but we had a new site now, and we weren't going to be stopped again. We began having meetings with the planning board, where we made the presentations of our plans, and gave everybody a copy of the résumés of our staff. We did this so that the board could feel comfortable in knowing that our staff were top professionals in their respective fields. I always felt that those presentations were most impressive. I'd give a brief outline of our intentions, and then I'd call upon individual members of the staff to go into their respective areas of concern—sanitation, security, protection of private property, engineering, logistics, etc.

Janis Joplin

We had everything documented, mapped out, and it was all covered quite thoroughly. By the time we had completed our presentation, if they weren't just blown away by it, then they just weren't listening.

The political thing started to happen again. We had to go to another meeting to find out what happened to the water permit. They weren't granting permits! I had to start work rebuilding the stage that day, and this was a 1:00 A.M. session called by the Bethel Town Council. I was sitting down on the steps of the Town Hall with Mel Lawrence, right under the flag, just looking up at it. You know how you can get hit by things—a whole wave of American history and American spirit—what's right and what's wrong; the whole thing kind of waved over us. I put my faith in that spirit, and Mel did too. It may sound corny, but that's the way we felt. I also remembered that

you really had to get out there and wail. That was my Brooklyn background.

Artie had been working the city and making a deal to film the festival. We both knew how important the film was going to be. The Monterey film was not a big success, but Artie and I felt this one would be. Artie had been sending film people to the site, and we had spoken to people at Paramount and various other distribution companies, but none of them really knew what we were doing. "Who's Jimi Hendrix and what's a Grateful Dead?" they'd ask.

I hired a film crew, Mike Margetz and Malcolm Hart, to come and shoot some of the construction preparations. Joel felt that with all we had to deal with, filming was the last thing we should be concerned with and took this as a personal insult. "Michael is making a film about himself while Rome is burning all around us." In my opinion that was not quite the case. We knew how important it was to document what was going on. In any case, we couldn't find anyone willing to put up $900,000 to shoot the film. We'd been talking with Mike Wadleigh and Bob Maurice and the Maysle Brothers about shooting. I wanted Wadleigh to shoot the acts and the stage and have the Maysle Brothers shoot the crowd. Wadleigh decided that he definitely wanted to shoot it even if he had to do it on credit, which was exactly the way he did shoot it. Artie finally worked out and signed a deal with Warner Bros. on Thursday before the festival. It was a 50–50 deal, with an advance of $100,000 for production costs and another $500,000 for editing. We had gone to everybody, honest to God, to sell it for $60,000, just to get it on film. Thinking back, it would have been great if we had shot it ourselves.

Peter Goodrich, my friend from Miami, was handling concessions and food. He talked to all kinds of food organizations, such as Horn and Hardart, Nedick's, Nathan's,—they wouldn't go for it. It was too big. Horn and Hardart did put together box lunches, but they were only for the crews. We found people who catered other festivals, but they turned us down because of previous experience with riots.

Peter found Jeff Jager who ran an antique shop called Second Hand Rose in Greenwich Village. He had done some catering before with some of his friends, and they said they would be able to handle it. Since no one else seemed able to, we decided to go ahead with Jeff. They called the project, or at least their organization for the festival, "Food for Love." The "Food for Love" people did not have the money to finance the project themselves. We were in a tight spot, with no alternative, it seemed. So Joel and John and Artie and I decided we had to finance them. We would build their booths and install the plumbing and electricity. The plan was that they were to pay us back out of the principal proceeds, plus a percentage of the profits. One of their big problems was getting the money picked up because they were afraid of getting ripped off. They were talking about carrying .44s and forming "flying wedges" and finally decided to take the money out by helicopter.

The Friday morning of the festival, "Food for Love" wanted more money and threatened to pull out. Peter Goodrich got hot and hit Jeff. Before the fight could get started, Lenny Kaufman, one of the special security team, came over and broke it up. He was rather imposing, so it didn't take much effort on his part. It seemed that "Food for Love" was trying to hold us up at the last minute, but finally we worked it out and the show went on.

We had the people who owned David's Potbelly, a restaurant in Greenwich Village, come up and handle the food for the performers. David was kind of a frantic character and was protecting his kitchen at the festival with a passion. But he did get everybody fed, not quite in the style he had envisioned, but fed nonetheless. The meals for the field staff were Peter Goodrich's responsibility, but during the last week before the festival

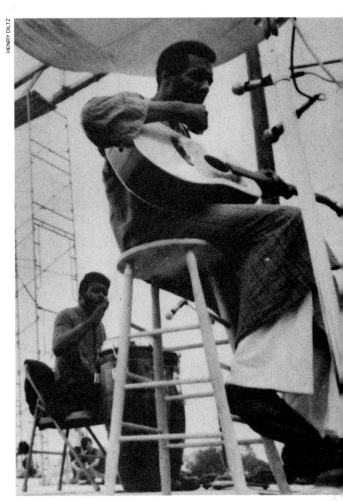

Richie Havens

Joan Baez

21

Peter started dropping out of sight. He would get on his motorcycle and ride off into the sunset. I don't know how he did it, but when the festival was happening, he somehow managed to get the 400 to 500 people working around the remote areas of the grounds served hot meals.

Peter had another critical job. He was in charge of the toilet facilities. During the planning stages he spent a lot of time at airports and bus terminals timing people as they went in and out of the johns. Taking an average time divided by 24 hours, multiplied by 300,000, he wound up with about 1,400 toilets, and it seemed to suffice.

There was not enough electrical power at Max's farm. We needed 220-volt lines and heavy cables to supply the power for the stage and lighting. At first, the electric company was going to charge us something like a million dollars to get the necessary eight-mile cable from the town of Bethel to the stage. Finally they decided that the people out in the county needed the added power anyway, so they charged us only overtime for their workers.

Backstage

The telephone and power guys got behind us and made an all-out effort to get the job done in time for the show. It was incredible to see their efforts.

We ran miles of new roads on Max's land. We gave them names like "Groovy Way" and "Happy Avenue." We also had to make access roads over all kinds of terrain so the trucks could get in and out to empty the johns and haul away the garbage.

I had some problems with Max getting him to go along with some of the things that we wanted to do. For

Backstage

example, we wanted to bury the plastic pipe that was going to be the "city's" water supply. Max wouldn't let us, so it stayed on top of the ground and broke frequently during the festival. Since the system was on a single pressure line, when one pipe broke the pressure for the whole system was down until it was fixed. A lot of the water was coming from White Lake itself. The lake is large, but I understand it dropped about 12 inches during the weekend of the festival. We were pumping it out through purifying systems, using tons of chlorine. Gene Mayer, one of Chris Langhart's crew, did the plumbing. We also machine-drilled six or seven wells that went down 60 feet or so with leased portable pumps. The man who owned the water rights to the lake was a man named Ben Leon. He was about 80 years old but had an incredible spirit. He gave us tremendous headaches because at first he wanted something like $1 a gallon for the water that we had taken from the lake; but eventually we came to an agreement with him, and we actually became quite good friends.

There was also Mr. Filipino, who owned some fields overlooking the lake and the roof behind the stage. As the festival was growing near, I realized that we were going to need more campgrounds. I went up to his house to talk to him about leasing his fields for camping purposes. We sat down and he offered me some of his homemade wine, and I got ripped. It was Joel who finally made the deal with him for $6,000 for the camping rights for the three days. That was Thursday night. Friday morning at about

Tim Hardin

5:00 A.M. we opened the campground. By the time the sun came up and Filipino woke up, there were people as far as you could see in his fields. Two kids were making it on his front steps, and he called us for help. We came up to his house and offered to take him to a hotel for the weekend, but he wouldn't leave. So we posted a guard on his porch. Finally, he got into what was happening and started asking people inside.

Canned Heat

About 12 volunteer Hog Farmers had come out early by bus to help set up the campgrounds and clear some of the land. The rest arrived two weeks before the festival, and they set up all the free kitchens and the storage areas for the food supplies. I think the presence of the Hog Farmers had a lot to do with the success of the festival. They ended up handling the freak-out cases and in general generating a good feeling among everyone they came in contact with. Wavy is a unique human being, totally selfless in all of his dealings with people, and his spirit was infectious.

Now we were rolling; everything seemed to be proceeding on schedule. The stage was going up, water systems were being laid out, electrical lines tied in, bridges, booths, roads, supply lines—all nearing completion. We had to get permits for everything. We had most of them signed two days before the show. The Town Council was sitting on them. They had agreed to issue the permits, but they didn't want to. I think it was close to election time and nobody wanted to get hung with the responsibility. At one point they had a warrant out for my arrest because we were operating all that time without permits. So I stayed among the Hog Farmers, avoiding having the warrant served on me, and for a while I ran things with a walkie-talkie from campground areas. We never did get permits to build a bridge for the performers to use to get to the stage. We just wrote out our own. We gave it to one of the guys and asked him to sign it, and he did.

There were people around who could paint, and they painted the bridge. It looked great.

Albert Grossman came up to the site about a week before the festival with Rick Danko. He was looking around with a "something's wrong" expression. Albert growled, "You know, you'll never be finished in time," and he was almost right. But I'd say that he had been one of the few managers who believed from the beginning that we were going to pull it off. He came to the show and seemed to enjoy it quite a bit.

We had planned to have a circus and to have arts-and-crafts areas and art shows. We had to cancel many of these peripheral activities when we left Wallkill because we didn't have time to prepare for them properly. The people were there, but they ended up in campgrounds mostly. Consequently, the arts part of the Music and Art Fair suffered somewhat.

Chris Langhart and Steve Cohen, with the help of Jay Drevers, oversaw the building of the stage. The construction crews did an incredible job getting as much done as they did in the three and half weeks we had to get ready. We built a revolving deck, which was a great idea, but the rain caused some problems with the wheels turning the deck on the stage, and it only revolved through the first day. Five huge tresses were built and were supposed to be flown over the stage. Fabric was to be stretched over these tresses and lighting bridges were to go under them. In case of rain the whole thing would be covered and well lit. Unfortunately, the tresses were so big that we had to wait for good weather to fly them, and we had to bring in two huge cranes to do it. They didn't get up until the day before the show started, so we ended

Mountain

up by putting canvas under it and the lights never got up at all. We did all the lighting from the towers out in front of the stage. All in all, it was very impressive-looking.

It is hard to imagine the pressure everyone was under during those last few days. It was apparent to all of us that hundreds of thousands of people were coming. The final hours of preparation were a monumental task, and everybody in a position of responsibility felt that it was all resting on his or her shoulders. To a degree it was true. It took all the energy from each one of us to get done in time for that weekend, and everyone concerned should feel proud of that effort. By the time we were supposed to be opening the gates there were already a couple of hundred thousand people out in the field. Someone suggested that we pass a basket, but I said it's not going to happen. If they hadn't already bought a ticket it was a free show.

The next thing was to get the show started. We checked everything out because it had rained Friday morning. The sound system gave us very little trouble. It was miraculous under those conditions.

I had laid out the schedule of appearances for everyone so the show would build over the three days. Richie Havens opened the show on Friday, followed by Joan Baez, John Sebastian, Arlo Guthrie, Tim Hardin, Melanie, Incredible String Band, Sweetwater, and Ravi Shankar. The performers on Saturday and Sunday were Credence Clearwater Revival; Sly and the Family Stone; Canned Heat; Grateful Dead; Jefferson Airplane; Janis Joplin; Santana; Mountain; The Band; Paul Butterfield; Blood, Sweat and Tears; Crosby, Stills, Nash and Young; Jeff Beck Group; Joe Cocker; The Moody Blues; The Who; Johnny Winter; and Jimi Hendrix.

All of the groups' sets were quite long; most of them were about an hour and a half each. Joe Cocker did two hours. Jimi Hendrix wanted to close the show because usually the headliner does close the show. His manager, Michael Jeffries, insisted; I said, "Listen, it's not like that. They're all headliners. Why don't you go on around midnight?" Jeffries said no, Hendrix had to close the show; so I said, "Okay. You got it," even though I knew it was not really a great spot to have, waiting up all night and knowing many of the people would have left already. On Monday morning, Hendrix did play an incredible set, but by the time he got to the stage there were only about 60,000 people left. The Jefferson Airplane had requested to play at dawn with the sun coming up behind them. But the schedule was rather rocky, so they ended up playing around 9:00 or 10:00 in the morning.

Even with all these big acts around there really wasn't a groupie thing backstage because everyone was either making music or listening to it. We also kept backstage clear so we could work. There was tight security on photographers because the film crew was shooting continually, and we didn't want them shooting a lot of photographers!

One of Artie's jobs was to walk the acts over to the stage, across the flying bridge, and explain to them, during that walk, about the filming that was going on. He told them to expect the cameras and explained that we didn't want anybody to be surprised by them because there had not been camera crews at most of the festivals they had played before. Some of the groups had signed permissions previously. Others signed within a few days after the festival. I don't think I ever signed a release for myself in the film; I don't think they needed it.

We booked The Iron Butterfly, which turned out to be a mistake because they had caused several riots over the summer. When they called up the site from the airport and said they weren't coming because we hadn't sent the helicopter, it was the best news I had heard in weeks. They said, "Where's our helicopter?" and I said, "Well, maybe next year."

In contrast, I really wanted Tim Hardin to be at the festival. I figured Woodstock could be Tim's big break. I had told him about it months and months before and he really got excited about it, but when he got to the site he got wasted and did a disappointing set. It was a shame.

Several acts got a real boost playing at Woodstock. It was Crosby, Stills, Nash and Young's second gig. David Crosby told me how he had arrived in a helicopter

thinking he was hallucinating. "The copter started to spin as we were coming into the site. I started to see all these people. We just roared down to the ground thinking the whole thing was a dream."

Actually things were constantly going on behind the scenes even during the performances. We didn't have any certified checks because we had expected to have cash on hand to pay the balance of the deposit to some of the acts before they went on. But there wasn't any gate: There wasn't any cash. As a matter of fact, when the Wells Fargo guy finally got through the crowd and appeared at

The Who

David Clayton Thomas of Blood, Sweat and Tears

our trailer, we told him to go home. It had taken him a day and a half to get his truck through all those crowds, so he just decided to stay until the end of the show.

I had sent Rocky Williams backstage to get The Who and the Grateful Dead ready to perform—to locate everyone so we would know where they were. We were trying to keep three acts ahead of ourselves. The rain was going to break. Rocky told me that The Who's manager was very uptight about getting paid, and Mickey Hart's father, who was managing the Grateful Dead, said they would not play unless they got a certified check. I said, "Don't they know it's Sunday and we don't have any cash today?" Still, they came down to the trailer, sat there on the grass, and they repeated their demands. I told them that we were in a real bind for cash, but I would give them a check now and they could go right to the bank Monday morning and cash it, and it would be good. In the meantime, I asked somebody to call Joel and tell him what was going on. Joel was constantly on the fringe. I was getting emotional, as both the manager of The Who and the manager of the Grateful Dead were becoming unreasonable. There was no way we could get them cash on the spot in time for them to go on. Finally, it dawned on me how to get these guys to let their acts play. I knew that the Grateful Dead really wouldn't be a problem; they were going to play no matter what. But The Who, on the other hand, I figured wouldn't play, so I told the manager, "Wait here. I'm going to go out and make an announcement that The Who is not going to play until they get the cash and we'll see how that goes over with the crowd." I guess that did the trick, because they played. In the meantime, Joel was getting the banker from White Lake out of bed and dragging him to the bank to get some checks certified. They arrived later that night. The Grateful Dead and The Who were the only two groups who created that kind of a problem, and everybody who performed at the festival got paid.

There were lots of social—or should I say antisocial—groups at the festival. The Motherfuckers came up from New York City. They were from the East Village in Manhattan, and their claim to fame was running through the streets smashing garbage cans. Their trip was just being antieverything. One guy was running around backstage screaming, "Tear down the gates, tear down the gates!" trying to incite people to some sort of action. He came up and started to argue with me. I said, "Listen, there aren't any gates." The guy didn't want to hear it; that didn't seem to matter to him. So one of our security guards removed him.

Another touch-and-go situation was Abbie Hoffman. He had just spent 22 hours working in the festival hospital and had flipped out. He had taken too much acid and was hallucinating, seeing people running around with guns and knives. At one point Abbie had me looking for a character with a gun under the stage. We were looking for the guy and Abbie turns to me and said, "You know, you're really not afraid to die." "Oh," I said, "let's go cool out a little bit, Abbie, and listen to the music." The Who were on stage and we started to watch their show. Abbie said, "I'm going to go out there and grab that microphone." I said, "Abbie, don't do it. It's not the right time or place for it." He kept saying, "I have to, I have to." I kept saying, "You can't, you can't." But he jumped up and grabbed the microphone and started to yell something about John Sinclair, who had been jailed for smoking a joint. Pete Townsend swung around and hit him with the top neck of his guitar while he was playing. Abbie jumped off the stage, over the fence, and disappeared into the crowd. It was very dramatic the way he did it. Later, he went to the White Lake Hospital and registered as Michael Lang and told everybody he was taking over the hospital!

Stanley Goldstein was crisis-oriented. He was always cool in the face of chaos, but when there wasn't a crisis to solve, Stanley would create one in his head. He was campground coordinator. He was like the General Patton of Woodstock. He would call up and sound like he was behind enemy lines. He'd say some group from the East Village was starting a ruckus. Then he'd call and say someone just stole his flashlight. Then he'd call and say somebody just stole his heater. Every hour he'd call and

Arlo Guthrie

Johnny Winter

say something else was gone. Finally, he called and said everything was gone. "This is going to be my last communication!"

There were half a million people around, and there were any number of potential disasters that could have occurred. Before the weekend started there was a lot of doom talk from some people, but it never got to me. I maintained a positive attitude through the whole thing. I just knew it was going to work, and this seemed to help sway the opinions of those around me. During the festival, if someone freaked out, we'd talk about it and usually I'd be able to cool them out. I remember Mel called in one day (I think it was the first day of the show) and said that everyone was laying the responsibility on him and he was having to support the whole operation. I said, "Mel, everyone here feels that way every time someone brings them a problem. It's a very critical time and there's a lot of

The Band

Richard Manuel

Rick Danko

Levon Helm and Robbie Robertson

pressure for everyone and we all just have to hold up our end. If you hang in everything will be fine." Mel got a grasp on things again and went back and did a beautiful job. I just tried to keep everyone going and they did keep going. Saturday afternoon I got this message from John Morris: "We've got to stop the show," he said. "I just talked to Joel and was convinced there would be a holocaust." John and Joel did not know what to think, not being on the site. They had no grasp of what was going on. It was much too fast and far away from them. They were getting paranoid. I told John that he had to be crazy to think that we could stop the show at that point. It would have been like stopping a Super Bowl game at half time and telling the crowd they had to go home.

There were water-main breaks. There was an increasing need for more doctors and helicopters. The doctors were always coming out saying we need more of this or more of that. Then the Army got involved because we needed more helicopters. I don't know how many kept coming in from the Army, certainly more than we needed, and we were very grateful for their help. Most people didn't know that there was a National Guard platoon standing by in Albany with helicopters filled with tear gas, in case the crowd got out of hand. But they saw that the plan was not feasible. The National Guard was bivouacking nearby, and the mud was everyplace you went. Omnipresent. Walking in it, sitting in it, everywhere. I can still smell it—it became the fifth element.

During the food-shortage scare Wavy announced from the stage, "Breakfast in bed for five hundred thousand." We had huge supplies for the free kitchens, so there was enough food for everyone, and everyone shared.

There was an announcement from the stage that we were considered a disaster area. It was announced as a joke. Artie and I did an interview from the stage with a TV commentator. He was petrified. He wanted to know what was going on, what did everybody think. I said, "Why don't you go out and talk to the kids in the crowd?" He said, "You want me to get down into *that?*"

That weekend was an eternity for me. It was a realization of all the things I had been working for and praying for—all coming true. Somehow all of us working together and living together had come through together.

By the time the festival was over most of our equipment was missing—cars, walkie-talkies, motorcycles! There were farmers who pulled up and rolled our fencing right up into their trucks. We found well pumps gone, pieces of pipe, pieces of the stage, just anything that could move.

Monday morning I had gotten a call to meet John, Joel, and Artie in the city. I went to say goodbye to some of the guys and left in a helicopter; the pilot was giving me a free ride into the city. It was the first time I had seen the sight from the air, as I had never gotten up to see it during that weekend. There was garbage everywhere. The Hog Farmers had made a peace sign out of some of the debris.

The next thing I remembered was landing at Wall Street at the heliport. It was a weird feeling. An incredible contrast to what I had just lived through. By the time I got to the bank there had been a blowup between Artie Kornfeld, Artie Ripp, Albert Grossman, Joel, and John. Albert wanted to buy out Joel's and John's part of Woodstock Ventures. He knew the film was going to work and that there was a lot of value in the corporate name at that point. He made an offer, taking John's family off the hook. John was outraged at that point and didn't want to do anything more. Joe Vigoda, a music-business lawyer, was there at that meeting at the bank. It was bizarre. Everyone was screaming and at odds with one another. Nothing was resolved, and I went back up to the site to make sure that the cleanup was proceeding.

I stayed for about a day and again I had to go back to the city. On my way in I picked up some money at a local ticket outlet—about $30,000. I drove to Joel's and John's apartment, where they continued to ask if I wanted Artie out, and when I said no, Joel went off the wall. Woodstock Ventures was reported to be $1,300,000 in the hole at that point, and we talked about ways of working it out. I told Joel that I had $30,000 in the car and if he went downstairs with me I'd give it to him. Joel was almost incoherent at that point.

The next day we went back to our attorney's office to discuss dissolution of Woodstock Ventures. We proceeded on the basis that either they would buy our shares out or we would buy theirs. My interest was not in getting out

Crosby, Stills, Nash and Young

Neil Young

Graham Nash and David Crosby

but in getting Woodstock out of debt. We made a settlement a few days after that. We would take Joel and John out of the picture by assuming all of the debts and paying them $150,000, or they would take us out of debt and pay us $75,000. I wasn't really concerned with the number at that point because I really wanted to take them out, but I never figured out why it was $150,000 for them and only $75,000 for us. We wanted to get an accounting so we could show our position to people who had been interested in putting up money. Besides Albert, Artie Ripp had found a few other people, and it seems as though we would be able to raise the money we needed. In addition, Artie and I had gone to Warner Brothers to see Fred Weintraub to try and get him to give us an advance on the film so that we could at least take the corporation out of its immediate problems and pay the things we had to pay. Weintraub said no, he didn't think the film was a very good risk at that point, and so he was unwilling to give us any money. That was what Freddie was saying.

Since Warners had turned us down it came down to one alternative: Artie and I had to sell to Joel and John because no accounting was forthcoming and the pressure from John's father to take the corporation into bankruptcy was getting heavier all the time. I had had enough of the arguments and the hassle and the resentment that was being built up, so Artie and I decided to leave. But shortly after we did, Warner Brothers reportedly paid one million dollars to Woodstock Ventures for the rights to the film.

I wonder whether Warners might have held out until they could deal solely with John and Joel.

I understand that Warners has made about $35,000,000 on the film and many more millions on the records. In fact, by buying Woodstock they made their first coup in many years. It got them out of the hole that they were in, and they began making money off the youth culture. Sometime in 1974 a friend of mine had asked to see the film, and so I called Warners and asked them if I could get a copy of the 16mm print. They said sure, and after about a year and a half they finally got it to me and sent me a bill for $600.

Looking back, I think that one of the major factors in the festival's success was that it happened spontaneously, and so folks had to react to it naturally. There was no precedent for social behavior while "living with 500,000 friends." I think we projected the right feeling for the event all through its preparation, and the people who were there carry this feeling with them to this day.

For me, Woodstock, from conception to completion, was a wonderful experience. I think that's true for all of us who worked on it, something that we will always cherish. I've been asked repeatedly about doing another Woodstock, but I think the festival was a unique event, and to try to repeat it would be a mistake. Times have changed, and new ideas should grow out of new times.

—Michael Lang

WOODSTOCK
MUSIC & ART FAIR

presents

AN
AQUARIAN
EXPOSITION
in
WHITE LAKE, N.Y.*

WITH

FRI., AUG. 15
Joan Baez
Arlo Guthrie
Tim Hardin
Richie Havens
Incredible String Band
Ravi Shankar
Sly And The Family Stone
Bert Sommer
Sweetwater

SAT., AUG. 16
Canned Heat
Creedence Clearwater
Grateful Dead
Keef Hartley
Janis Joplin
Jefferson Airplane
Mountain
Quill
Santana
The Who

SUN., AUG. 17
The Band
Jeff Beck Group
Blood, Sweat and Tears
Joe Cocker
Crosby, Stills and Nash
Jimi Hendrix
Iron Butterfly
Ten Years After
Johnny Winter

ART SHOW
Paintings and sculptures on trees, on grass, surrounded by the Hudson valley, will be displayed. Would-be artists, ghetto artists, and accomplished artists will be glad to discuss their work, or the unspoiled splendor of the surroundings, or anything else that might be on your mind. If you're an artist, and you want to display, write for information.

CRAFTS BAZAAR
If you like creative knickknacks and old junk you'll love roaming around our bazaar. You'll see imaginative leather, ceramic, bead, and silver creations, as well as Zodiac Charts, camp clothes, and worn out shoes.

If you like playing with beads, or improvising on a guitar, or writing poetry, or molding clay, stop by one of our work shops and see what you can give and take.

FOOD
There will be cakes and hotdogs and dozens of curious food and fruit combinations to experiment with.

HUNDREDS OF ACRES TO ROAM ON
Walk around for three days without seeing a skyscraper or a traffic light. Fly a kite, sun yourself. Cook your own food and breathe unspoiled air. Camp out: water and latrines will be supplied. Tents and camping equipment will be available at the Camp Store.

MUSIC STARTS AT 4:00 P.M. ON FRIDAY, AND AT 1:00 P.M. ON SATURDAY AND SUNDAY.

It'll run for 12 continuous hours, except for a few short breaks to allow the performers to catch their breath.

AUGUST 15, 16, 17.

One day $7.00 Two days $13.00 Three days $18.00

For tickets and information write to:
WOODSTOCK MUSIC
BOX 996, RADIO CITY STATION
NEW YORK 10019

*White Lake, Town of Bethel, Sullivan County, N.Y.

3 DAYS of PEACE & MUSIC

Skolnick

Center: Michael Lang, Right: John Morris

HENRY DILTZ

HENRY DILTZ

Chip Monck

Mel Lawrence

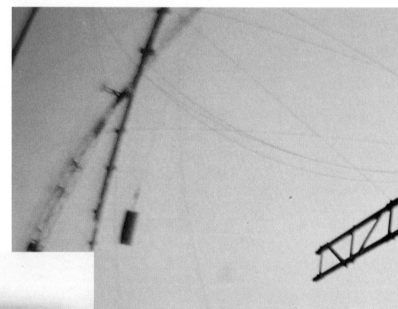

Wavy Gravy and Michael Lang

Center: Peter Goodrich

HENRY DILTZ

HENRY DILTZ

HENRY DILTZ

Tisha Bernuth

39

Backstage construction

Construction of concession stands

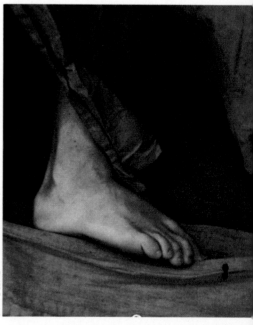

The road to the festival

BARRY Z. LEVINE

The playground

Wavy Gravy, Abbie Hoffman,
and Paul Krasner

Security guards

The Hog Farm

HENRY DILTZ

Swami Satchidananda

Rose of the Incredible String Band

Richie Havens

58

Janis Joplin

ELLIOTT LANDY

HENRY DILTZ

HENRY DILTZ

The Bridge

Grace Slick

Performers and crew backstage

64

Max Yasgur

Joe Cocker

Greg Erico of Santana

Jerry Garcia of the Grateful Dead

FOR RENT

Bob 'The Bear' Hite
of Canned Heat and
John Sebastian

Opposite: Tim Hardin
and Richie Havens

John Sebastian

Sweetwater

Sha-Na-Na

Melanie

Arlo Guthrie

Joan Baez

Ravi Shankar

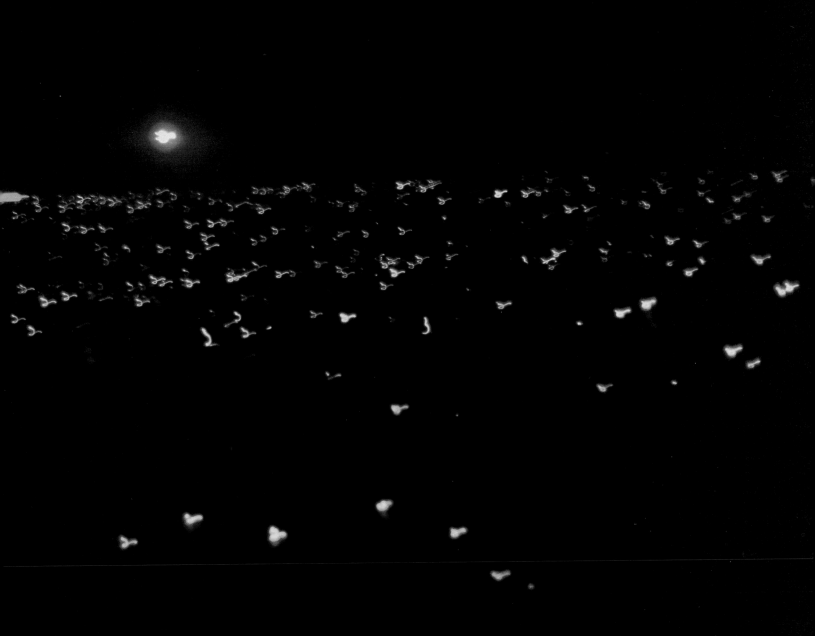

Jerry Hyman, Lew Soloff, and Chuck Winfield

Blood, Sweat and Tears

David Clayton Thomas

Janis Joplin

Creedence Clearwater Revival

John Fogarty

Doug Clifford

Mountain

Leslie West

Felix Pappalardi

Canned Heat

84

Stu Cook and Tom Fogarty of Creedence Clearwater Revival

ELLIOTT LANDY

HENRY DILTZ

LEE MARSHALL

Jerry Garcia and Bob Weir of The Grateful Dead

Sly Stone

Opposite: Roger Daltrey of The Who

The Band

Levon Helm

Rick Danko, Robbie Robertson, and Richard Manuel

Stephen Stills, David Crosby, and Graham Nash

HENRY DILTZ

ELLIOTT LANDY

Johnny Winter

Grace Slick and the Jefferson Airplane

BARRY Z LEVINE

HENRY DILTZ

Jimi Hendrix

Talk to people who were there, and as they think back, their voices, their eyes, everything about them changes. They become totally animated, as if they were recalling some mystical event. Something unprecedented did happen in that coming together: The Woodstock Festival was the greatest spontaneous social event of the epoch. To varying degrees of intensity, it was an event that changed the lives of almost all who participated in it.

What happened there? Why did the Woodstock Festival embody a mystical quality—a psychic coming together? What was the Aquarian chemistry that brought all the related, yet disparate, elements of a counterculture to a point, an apex of the Sixties?

Looking back ten years later, I find it easier now to analyze the festival. It wasn't something that just happened and then passed into oblivion. It left its mark. The Encyclopedia Britannica contains an article on it; "Woodstock Generation" is defined in Webster's Dictionary; and the comic strip *Peanuts* has a character called Woodstock.

By now the Woodstock Generation has integrated—sometimes subtly, often flagrantly—whatever it was they experienced into the mainstream of American life. Yet some of that generation, who were a real part of the great spirit of change in the Sixties, now feel estranged from the flow of culture. For those who lived through that unusual era, living since then has not had quite the same momentous force, and the Woodstock experience is all the more treasured as a result. After all, if you had passed

WOODSTOCK:
Looking Back

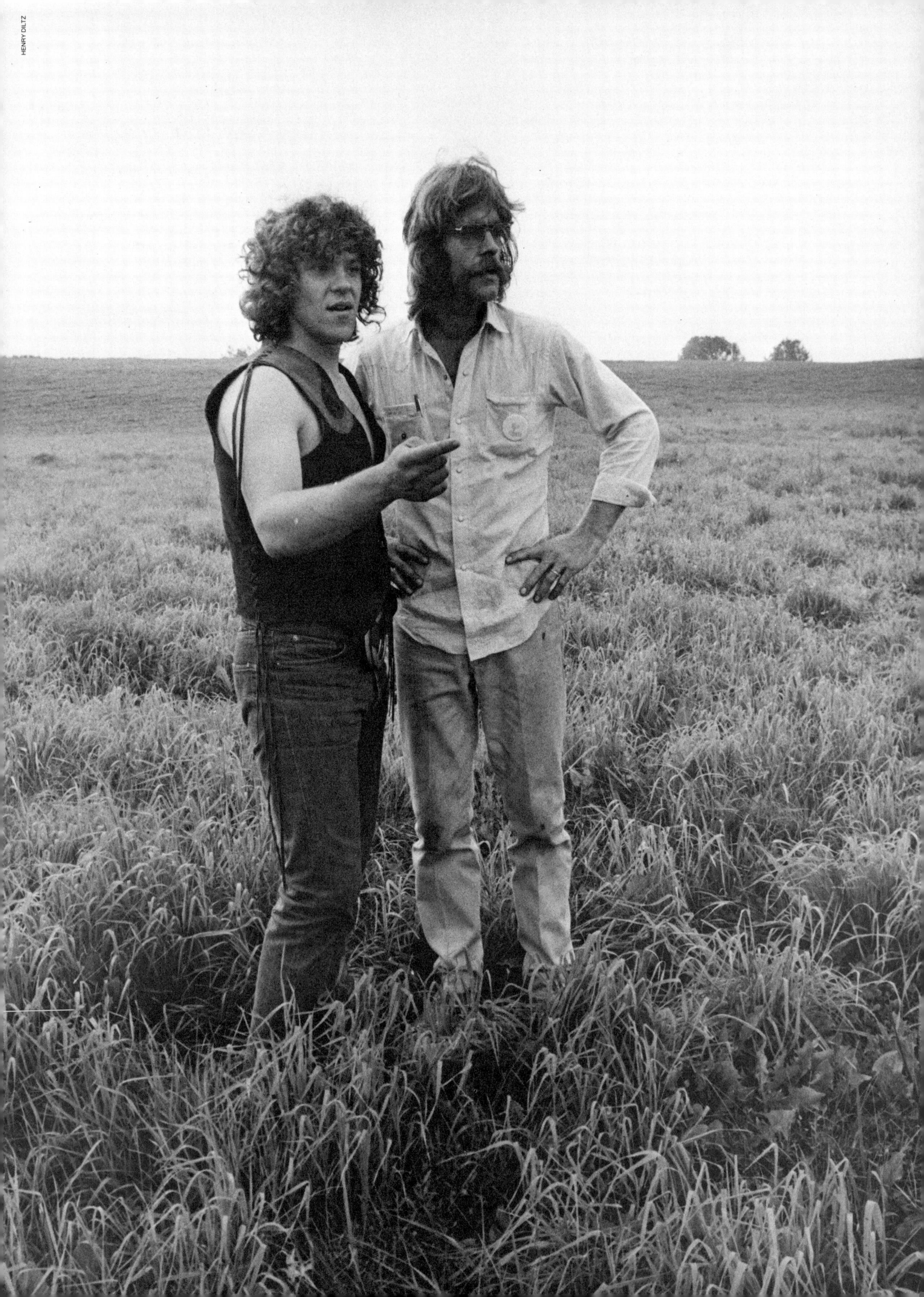

HENRY DILTZ

your youth in an age of moon landings, political uprisings, black power, civil-rights struggles, psychedelics, rock music, and innovative lifestyles, the Seventies *would* seem quiet.

The years prior to the festival were filled with turmoil: Jack Kennedy, Martin Luther King, and Bobby Kennedy were assassinated. There was the Vietnam war. There were flower power, black power, progressive political movements, and the uprisings at Berkeley and Columbia. There was the Chicago Democratic Convention, where TV viewers watched young Americans brutally beaten by Mayor Edward Daley's police.

By the time of the Woodstock Festival, Oriental philosophies (Zen in particular), interest in the occult and astrology (all underground concerns of the Fifties) were no longer obscure. They were very popular with the youth. Alan Watts and Hermann Hesse were more than esoteric names. Even Adele Davis had finally attained popularity with her very early books on health, vitamins, and organic food. There was the outburst of acid rock, the psychedelicizing of the youth of the country by Tim Leary and Dick Alpert, and the idolizing of Bob Dylan, who had gone electric in '66.

The Beatles (*Sergeant Pepper* appeared two years before the festival), the back-to-the-land and natural lifestyle movements, and the search for universal brotherhood—love and peace—by the flower people in Haight-Ashbury were all tremendously important social and cultural movements. Nonconformity erupted in the Sixties; there were new ways of looking at religion, health care, drug experimentation, civil rights, and the Vietnam war. Rock music infiltrated the pop-music mainstream on the AM wavelength. Broadcast first on FM radio, it was an early voice of the counterculture. Music was overwhelming the other art forms, such as painting and literature, and it hooked the artistically inclined youth because of its vitality. All these divergent, unrelated aspects of the social forces shaping those years were converging. The time and place they coalesced was on August 15, 16, and 17, 1969, at the Woodstock Music and Art Fair.

That summer the festival promoters put out two giant signals, a kind of cosmic announcement: first, the acts appearing presented the full range of music popular with that generation; second, it was going to be happening in the country—Bob Dylan's country. You could party there for three whole days!

The music was a rallying call. There were more top acts scheduled to play than had ever been gathered before at a rock concert. A wide variety of music was offered. Ravi Shankar, at the peak of his popularity, symbolized both the religious and Indian influences; Richie Havens, Joan Baez, and Arlo Guthrie represented the protest and folk aspects of the culture; and Tim Hardin was part of the folk-rock movement. Country music had come into the major rock scene simultaneously with the back-to-the-land movement (Dylan had just made *Nashville Skyline*). Just about everyone playing at the festival, except the hard-rock acts, had a touch of country in their music. The Blues were not forgotten. Among others there were the

Opposite: Michael Lang with Chip Monck
Above: Michael with Linda Kornfeld

Paul Butterfield Blues Band and Joe Cocker, who had had a recent successful appearance at the Fillmore East. Psychedelic and hard-rock greats like The Who (*Tommy* had just sold over two million copies) and Jimi Hendrix were featured. Hendrix's interpretation of "America the Beautiful," which closed the festival, embodied most musical styles and was an almost simultaneous musical expression of the festival itself. There was nothing sentimental or mainstream-middle-American about any of it. Besides the music, the setting of the festival had its appeal. It was happening in the countryside, just when the back-to-the-land movement was in full flower. People were experimenting with communal living, and be-ins had become nationwide and socially important events. Also, those who had been to bluegrass and folk festivals and knew what it was like to camp out were drawn to the festival. They all came prepared. They all came counting on having a good time.

Most people anticipated the kind of crowd that would be there; they knew who would be attracted to the music and to the scene. Many gurus, prophets, vagabonds, jugglers, and clowns came. They knew they could show their lifestyles freely, and they would be accepted and even approved. They could act as flamboyantly as they liked.

From all over kids came to join with people of their own kind to have a good time. It was to be an occasion free of ridicule, judgment, or criticism. Some, in just *wanting* to let their hair grow long or to wear brightly striped bell-bottom pants in school, had suffered through all kinds of flak. Some kids had been arrested, had left home, or

had been expelled from school because of these simple choices in style. Most had listened to the words of Dylan and the Beatles and were aware that the times were changing, aware of that even if they had only experienced this in small ways in their own home towns. What they read in the words "Three Days of Peace and Music in the Country" on the festival poster was *freedom!*

Kids 17 to 24 were just coming of age; they were the numerous offspring born in the postwar baby boom, the period of highest birth rate in American history, and they were the affluent, educated sons and daughters of those who had benefited by the economic expansion of the Fifties and Sixties. They could support the music they liked, and they could take off and go to the festival.

Woodstock was going to be a three-day *event*, not a one-day or one-night concert where the audience, crowded into a stadium, sits and listens while somebody onstage performs. The whole concept was different. At this festival the entire audience was camping out on a stage of its own. For three days they could leave behind jobs, girlfriends, boyfriends, parents, everything that was straight. They would come in decorated cars, vans, and buses; in tie-dye shirts, army fatigues, and saris; with books, bongos, and guitars; with wine and drugs— whatever their choice of lifestyle, they would be themselves. This was a place to share whatever it was that made them different. They were going to be an active part of the festival as much as the performers were.

The town of Woodstock, a crafts center in the beginning of the century, at the time of the festival was one of the few art colonies in the United States. It had been home to many artists, including Ash Can painters, WPA artists in the Thirties, and some abstract expressionists. The Art Students League of New York City had its summer school

in Woodstock. It had a playhouse, and there was also opera and Sunday-afternoon chamber music concerts. Woodstock had attracted the intellectual, liberal, and artistic types who either had independent incomes or were making it in the city. About 1964 Bob Dylan made his home there, and Dylan drew the new wave to Woodstock: folk and rock musicians, music-world business people, and all the supporting professions, from photographers to dealers. By the end of the Sixties many famous musicians and recording stars from the United States and England either had visited or summered at Woodstock or settled down there permanently. It was then that the older art-world contingent, who had been the major controlling force in Woodstock, began to feel the impact of the rock scene. Even the internationally recognized artists and writers living in Woodstock were at first perplexed by youth's noticeable adulation of rock music. Young people were not interested in established reputations in the rarefied worlds of painting, sculpture, and literature. Again, Woodstock was suddenly the center instead of the fringe of an artistic movement. This time it was rock music. The Woodstock Festival was the leavening of the lump, the coming together of the rock and hippie cultures. Before it, there had been significant festivals emphasizing music, such as Monterey, which launched Jimi Hendrix and Janis Joplin, and many more were scheduled around the country for the spring and summer of '69, but most people were not aware that there already was a rock-music celebration in the Woodstock area called the Woodstock Sound Festival. It had been held outdoors every summer since 1967 in the town of Saugerties, ten minutes from Woodstock. It was started and run by Pam Copeland on her defunct farm. People could not only drive a van in, but they could also set up tents and camp out. In the Sound Festival's first year, The Blues Magoos, who had just come off a United States tour with The Who, were the big attractions. They had rented a house in Woodstock. The Mothers of Invention, who also lived in Woodstock, played at the farm, along with Van Morrison, Peter Walker, Cat Mother, The Colwell Windfield Blues Band, Fear Itself with Ellen McIlvaine, Chrysalis, Children of God, and Jim Black (Omar), a congo drum player from the West Coast. Bob Fass from New York radio WBAI emceed. Later on, in '68, Tim Hardin, who was at his peak, moved to Woodstock and played at the festival, as did Major Wiley, The Crow Dog Indian Dancers, Rebecca and Sunny Brook Farmers, Chickie Neubles River Band, and The Pentacle Light Show. The Sound Festival lasted through the summer of 1970 when James Taylor, Elephants Memory, and Soft Machine (now the Electric Light Orchestra) played in Woodstock.

The idea for the Woodstock Aquarian Festival began with Michael Lang and Artie Kornfeld. Although they were by most standards young and eccentric, they were both already entrepreneurs of the new culture. Artie was an executive in a recording company, and Michael had already promoted the Miami Pop Festival. They knew that to get things done you didn't just dream about them or talk about them—you had to put your ideas into action; you had to spend money.

Michael Lang was 22 when he came up from Miami with a group of people following him. Among the group were the late Peter Goodrich (a sort of underworld mentor to the Miami counterculture and connoisseur of pre-Colombian art), his two teenagers, and Sonia, Michael's "lady," all of whom lived in a rented converted barn in Woodstock. (Michael was, for all practical purposes, New York City-based and made his personal appearances mostly on weekends.) Peter had worked with Michael on the Miami festival and apparently had a great influence on Michael's attitudes. Together they nurtured a plan to have a restaurant in Woodstock surrounded by a sculpture garden and featuring live music. Himself a sculptor in his free time, Michael, like many in the Sixties, was into the visual experience. He had sold the then innovative Art Nouveau-influenced posters that were coming out of San Francisco, as well as records, in his Miami (Cocoanut Grove) head shop. In Woodstock, he became friends with Isaac Abrams, the psychedelic painter, and met The Band, whose first album, *Big Pink*, was recorded in Woodstock. Michael's interest in both the artists and the musicians of the area was a reflection of the times. People like the Rolling Stones, Jerry Garcia, David Bowie, John Lennon, Peter Townsend, and Peter Yarrow had all switched from painting to music. Attracted to the vitality of this music, the potential for experimentation, innovation, and creativity, perhaps more budding artists than in any other period turned from careers in the visual arts to a major involvement in music—and Michael was attuned to this change.

Construction of the playground

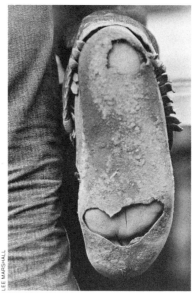

Michael became the Woodstock Festival's artistic director and its success was dependent on his psychology. He was the person who took both the credit and the blame for the festival, the central force that took hold of the luminous wheel that turned a dream fantasy into a historic reality. Michael's personality was exactly suited to dealing with the interactions and complexities necessary to make the festival happen in '69. Michael was so young—a combination of cherub, Pan, and satyr, with a halo of long, curly, light-brown hair. He was laid-back and not one to talk at great length. He was not a typical macho leader. Yet he was able to attract people to him, get the festival started, and keep it going.

One has to remember that the *youth* culture was at its peak: the Renaissance idealization of youth was again in full swing. It was a time when a 14-year-old was asked his or her *personal* opinion. Kids were important. They had power. They were pivotal.

Even so, Michael's achievements are impressive. Some people placed in his position might have copped out, but Michael seemed to blossom, striving for results that tested his own boundaries, that made maximum use of his potential. He possessed an enthusiasm, a youthful determination and, beyond that, a kind of fearlessness perhaps founded in a mystical experience he had had following an automobile accident. But the most striking of Michael's characteristics was his almost uncanny ability to think positively at all times. He seldom said anything negative about anyone, and so one got the feeling that perhaps he just didn't care that much. Or perhaps he just didn't have the time to be negative. He seemed to be detached, yet at the same time, quietly assertive, and probably this highly individualistic kind of aggressiveness was the basis for his successful leadership.

From the beginning, no matter how negative a particular situation might be, Michael always had a positive outlook and communicated this to his staff, calming them down, getting them to move in the right direction with his delivery of one-liners: "It's okay"; or "Don't worry, we'll work it out"; or "We've got that covered"; or "It's already gone down." This positive vibration had its effect. People were encouraged to be productive; things got done. The staff would come to him with ideas, and he'd say, "Get it together" or "Great. Go do it." He was the ideal sounding board for the ideas and talents and energy of those who worked around him. He was the executive, taking input from other people and making the festival his.

Taking on responsibility means a readiness to accept jabs, blame for slip-ups, and criticism for anything that could go wrong, or right. That willingness to accept such a huge responsibility, to assume a position marked by so many apparent uncertainties, separates Michael Lang from most people. It helped too that he had taken a major part in the Miami Pop Festival, and by the time he began to organize the Woodstock Festival, Michael had check-signing authority, which gave him great power. People knew that he had the experience and the means to put the festival together (he had connected with financial backers) and that he was taking *total* responsibility in directing the festival.

On the other hand, assuming responsibility implies leadership. Most people do not *want* responsibilities, and they *need* to be given *permission* to do things, to take care of problems, to build and create, to keep going. Michael was in this regard a no-hassle permission base. He

LEE MARSHALL

LEE MARSHALL

always underplayed everything—putting out little energy himself, while at the same time giving the other person all the freedom and all the rope he or she could possibly want. His attitude implied that other people would have to carry a lot of responsibility on their shoulders, too.

As confident and competent as he was, Michael didn't always face the facts. A co-worker at the festival said, "There's a part of Michael that cannot stand on his own two feet. At the same time, he stands on everybody's feet." While he assumed great responsibility, Michael could also be very evasive, to the point of being irresponsible. He dodged bill collectors and injunction servers, wrote his own permits, and told people things were under control when they weren't. Someone close to Michael commented, "He doesn't care about who he's dealing with. He will do anything to get what he wants." Perhaps such an attitude was necessary to maintain what is called an "overview." In any case, it was the quality that enabled Michael to hold back anything that might have stopped the festival, to persevere in the face of negative forces, and ultimately to realize his goal.

Michael was a master of passive assertiveness and delay, of assimilation and dissimilation, and he played the game out. It was important that he was also part of the essential feeling of the new age, along with Artie Kornfeld and the people on his staff. He was part of the rhythm of the Sixties, and that helped to explain why he knew how to play the game in the first place.

Michael's and Artie's partnership with the backers had two positive aspects. One, the fact that the festival backers themselves were very young—John Roberts was 24 years old, and his partner, friend, and lawyer, Joel Rosenman, was 23 years old—was consistent with Woodstock's youthful orientation. Second, the backers were not part of any corporate giant, such as Time, Inc., or NBC, or Warner Bros. (who eventually harvested the economic fruits the festival produced). Just out of college, each with a quick college-boy sense of humor and intelligence, John and Joel had already put together a recording studio (Media Sound in New York City) with the interest John was getting from a trust fund. At the time, they were far removed from the world of drop-outs, the streetwise, and the hip world of youth revolt. They knew, though, that the hippie culture was having a lot of fun, and they wanted to be in on it. Relative to their backgrounds, John and Joel were as unconventional as Michael and Artie, and they reinforced that sense of a festival by-the-people, for-the-people. All four of them had common entrepreneurial experiences in the youth market; all four thought they knew what appealed to it.

Michael and Artie became partners on a 50–50 basis with Joel and John. However, Michael, who for some time held Artie's shares, had to co-sign every check, which put him in command of the resources. The initial budget for the festival was $500,000. They were talking about a top gate, at first, of 100,000 tickets, and they didn't exceed the budget until late in the festival schedule. They felt the original figure would cover expenses until the ticket sales started coming in. It was primarily John's "big credit line in the sky," as Michael called it—money borrowed against his trust—that financed the project and kept it going.

Michael had very little money in the festival, and Artie had not much more.

Having the courage to be the leader and say, "Let me preside over this," Michael began to collect a staff. The first person he hired was Stanley Goldstein, who had worked with him in Florida. Michael felt that Stanley instinctively had a good feeling about the festival and knew how to seek things out. He was a good investigator and researcher. He got $500 a week, which at the time was a lot of money, and he started to bring people to Michael. It was Stanley Goldstein who convinced the Hog Farmers, a rural commune, to come from New Mexico to help at Woodstock. It was Stanley, too, who connected Michael and Tisha Bernuth, the woman who became his assistant.

Peter Goodrich, who had great public-relations skills, was another big help to Michael. He took everyone in—his eyes always sparkled—and he had many friends. People loved Peter.

Eccentric, iconoclastic, certainly nonconforming, Michael did not go to the conventional real-estate agents to find a site for the festival. Instead, he asked Jim Young, who owned a book and record shop in Woodstock, to look for a site, and he gave him an $800 retainer to do it. A 68-acre defunct golf course in Saugerties was the first location he showed to Michael, who turned it down. It was at the end of a dead-end road and almost inaccessible.

The next site was in the town of Krumville. The name was perfect. It wasn't just funky; it was *krummy*. An abandoned stock-car track right in the middle of an old farm, it could with effort accommodate 50,000 people. It was decided that it wouldn't be big enough. The Beatles had drawn 100,000 at Shea Stadium four years before,

and with all the acts (including Janis Joplin) Michael was talking about signing, the anticipated crowd would blow the whole house down. For sure, 100,000 seemed an underestimation.

Then there was a corn farm in Kerhonkson, forty minutes from the town of Woodstock, which would hold 60 to 100,000 people. The owners were straight country people who would have been outraged once they saw the long-haired hippies who had signed on as the festival crew. So when Michael brought his staff up to see this site, the main concern was to keep the owners and the crew from getting too close. The negotiations probably fell through because of the hostility between country lawyers and city lawyers.

The most perfect site—good access and hundreds of acres, right off the New York Thruway and other major arteries, and twenty minutes away from Woodstock—was in Saugerties. The owner, a sausage king, also had problems with the festival's lawyers and vice versa. From $5,000 (the original figure in the rent budget) they went to $40,000, which was the price asked for the Saugerties site.

After this location fell through, Joel and John found Wallkill. They took a ride upstate and went to the real-estate brokers. They finally hit an agency which dealt in industrial parks, land-zoned for industrial development. They saw Howard Mills's property and agreed on $10,000 for the use of his land for the festival, if they could get the approval of the zoning board. They took a $1,500 option.

Michael was working on many things simultaneously. He was bombarding Joel and John with the likes of Chip

Monck, the lighting genius from the Fillmore West and
Monterey Festival, and other technical experts and
geniuses of the alternate culture, such as Mel Lawrence,
who had worked as operations director at the festival. All
these people had been around for years, inventing and
improvising on the techniques that are now part of the
standard stage procedure used by touring groups
and in concerts.

  Michael could be an ambitious charmer; these giants of
rock technology worked for him. Had Michael taken any
one line and stuck with it, had he been loud and
demanding, he couldn't have gotten much accomplished.
His power was in his receptiveness; it was most conducive
to working with the dynamic people who created and built
the festival.

  Michael was talking about booking Janis Joplin and a lot
of the others when the Saugerties site was found in the
winter of '68. But by spring, while considering the Wallkill
site, he had signed almost everyone who was eventually
to perform. Michael instructed the booking agent to pay
double the standard fees for the first three acts he booked.
This strategy guaranteed everyone that the festival was for
real. His grasp of the psychology of superstars was right
on target. He guessed they would be status-conscious,
sensitive to hierarchy. He figured the others would want to
play the festival because a few big names had already
signed, and his shrewdness worked. The groups that were
signed later did not get the double fee. Michael felt they'd
perform for nothing just to be there.

Michael had a special wisdom. He anticipated all the various elements the festival needed to make it work. For instance, he was not concerned about whether the many technical people, eventually hired in large numbers, all had the right attitude about the project, as long as they did their jobs. However, those who were essential to the "feel" of the festival, such as Wes Pomeroy, the security chief (his duty was keeping the peace and not, Michael made sure, law enforcement), were screened basically for attitude. Wes had the right attitude, even though he came from "the Establishment" and had been coordinator of all law-enforcement agencies under Attorney General Ramsey Clark. Wes had also guarded VIPs such as the Beatles, and he was open and flexible.

The festival promoters came to an understanding with Wes Pomeroy that the security people would not carry weapons and would not be in uniform. They would wear informal attire—T-shirts, orange windbreakers, and safari helmets. Wes screened all applicants, eliminating hostile types and those with anti-youth prejudices. This concept of security discouraged violence and added to the right feel of the festival.

The second-string security force that sent out the right vibrations was the Hog Farmers. They worked well with everyone: with Pomeroy, with Dr. Abruzzie and the medical team; they manned the free-food kitchen and organized the camping grounds and the cleanup. Everyone who had anything to do with them, even Joel and John, said that the Hog Farmers under Hugh Romney (alias Wavy Gravy) set the right tone for the entire festival.

Joel and John called Wavy the real star of the festival. Tom Smuckers, in his essay "The Politics of Rock," said, "I ended up eating Hog Farm food (mainly grains) that was cheap and good, admiring their productivity and good vibes and comparing them to the politicians and their leaflets."

When it came to security, the Hog Farmers had an attitude that was not only imaginative but effective. It was part of the peace-and-love approach that had favorably influenced the confrontation with the police earlier that year on Easter morning at the Sheep Meadow be-in in New York's Central Park. People there had gone up to the mounted police with a wave of good feelings and open hands; it was like the flower stuck in the barrel of a gun. The Hog Farmers "flowered" their constraints with theatrics and humor, promoting pacifism. They called their security the *Please Force*. They believed you could stop a fight by throwing a pie, transforming a real fight into a different, less serious kind of fight. They had techniques for bringing people together, such as blowing up balloons for the crowd to bat into the air over and over again. Their peaceful attitude was the key to the festival.

After the apparent approval from the Wallkill Zoning Board, the staff started building the stage, planning out the site, and spending a lot of money on it. Rumor had spread quickly, and tickets were being sold before the ad campaign got underway. By then the booking was finished, the posters printed, and the announcements sent out—the first in mid-April, when the festival was

mentioned on New York's WNEW-FM. A major problem in getting outlets to sell the tickets had been the contract that Joel had drawn up. It was outrageous. The outlets—bookstores, head shops, record and leather shops—had to agree to a lien on everything they owned as security for the tickets they received. Before that, when there were only rumors that you could buy tickets in Woodstock shops, fans, not wanting to miss the festival, appeared in town, leaving money with shop owners and asking them to send the tickets when they came in.

Tickets cost $7 for one day, $13 for two days, and $18 for all three days. The contract was a common complaint among the outlets. When one bookshop owner told Joel how unreasonable it was, Joel replied, "You know, most of them [outlets] are going to be those head shops, and they just steal anything." But equally outrageous, the small print on the tickets absolved the promoters of all liability, even if the festival wasn't held. The tickets were two

months late in getting to some of the stores. By the time one Woodstock bookshop got its tickets, people had laid out about $1,000 in advance.

Two months later, on June 12, there was a meeting with the Wallkill Zoning Board, where the festival staff presented details of the plan, each member explaining his area of expertise to the board and the townspeople. By July 15, disc jockeys had created much excitement about the festival, and it was apparent by then that opposition at Wallkill was building up. Concerned citizens were just not

going to let the festival happen there. They felt threatened
when it became clearer to them that the crowd would be
larger than they had been led to believe, the music
wilder, and the audience . . . "marijuana smokers." At the
last meeting Michael and Tisha, his assistant, were sitting
behind a very large woman and her son, and suddenly
the woman said, "If one of those hippies comes on my
land, I'm going to shoot him, and I have a gun to do it!"
That was the end of that site. Soon after, they got a call
from the lawyer saying, "Forget it. You've got an
injunction." A few days later a call came in from White
Lake while Tisha was answering the phones. She
immediately called Michael at the lawyer's office, and,
with Mel Lawrence, they drove the 98 miles from the city
into the Catskills to the new site. It was a swamp. When
the owner started talking about dredging, they left. But
while driving around they saw a beautiful meadow: it was
Max Yasgur's 600-acre dairy farm. They met Max, who
agreed to rent it for $50,000.

As they were driving back from White Lake, Michael
told Tisha, "Listen, the negativity is a myth. This whole trip
that the world has gotta have wars and starvation . . . it's
a myth—everybody's riding on a myth. The next thing I
want to do is a world festival, just have a big party in the
world, and just all the youths of the world will get together
and celebrate. And then everyone will know it's a myth."

That night the trucks, loaded with equipment, were on
the road from Wallkill to White Lake. They had three
weeks to get the new site ready. A sign went up on Max
Yasgur's barn: "These are Max's cows. Please let them
groove," and that was pretty much the attitude of
everyone who arrived to set up the White Lake site. It was
fun and long hours, and it was a party. Even in the office
it was like a party, partly because Peter Goodrich was
always around with his asides such as, "Do you *know*
how many miles of hot dogs we need?" People worked 24
hours a day because of the good vibes and easy
cooperation. When the linemen from the phone and
electric companies came, even they got into the spirit of
getting the festival ready on time. The staff said it was like
having a house party—it was like the opening of the
house of the hippies. It became a celebration!

The Hog Farmers arrived two weeks early to help set
up. When John Roberts' father saw the photographs of
these "freaks" in the *New York Post* and read the covering
story saying they had arrived on a $17,000 chartered flight
to serve as an auxiliary security force for the festival, his
reaction, John writes in his book, was "What happened to
the police?" and "Are you out of your minds? . . .
Seventeen thousand dollars ! ! ? ?"

Other communes like the Ohayo Mountain Commune
in Woodstock arrived about that time also. The first teepee
was set up as a clearinghouse for everyone who came
to the site to help. Here they could find out where the help
was needed, where to eat and find water, and where to
camp. As groups arrived, they immediately would get the
feeling that this camp was very special. There was always
some job that needed to be done: laying paths, preparing
vegetables, setting up campsites and gathering stones
for fire pits, digging latrines, putting up fencing, cooking,

cleaning dishes and pots, and serving food to the crews, all of whom were given free meals. Before the workers would start in the morning, there would be yoga and breathing exercises, with hundreds joining in. Other groups would meditate. Everyone who was there remembers the high spiritual feeling among all those who helped set up the facilities.

In contrast to the people who came to work—to be an active part—Alan Gordon (who published *The Aquarian Angel* after the festival) came just to hang out. "Most people were into this 'doing' kind of thing," he said. "I wasn't into doing. I was just into wandering around the countrified area and chatting with people and watching this big panorama unfold in front of me. I didn't want to be nailed into one little corner of what was going on, so I didn't get heavy into doing."

Another group came early and played around with ideas for kids. They helped create the very successful playground. They piled bales of hay, and everyone jumped from a tree structure onto the haystacks. A tripod was erected with a tremendous rock weighing several tons suspended from it by ropes. Just under that swaying rock was another rock on the ground, and little kids would lie down between them and squeal in mock terror.

At the time of the festival, the new crafts movement was at its most innovative. Craftspeople in all fields came into the town of Woodstock before the festival, wanting to be part of the art fair. They wanted to have booths at the festival; and although Michael planned to have lots of crafts, ghetto artists, a circus, and posters as important

The Hog Farm

parts of the festival, there wasn't time to set it all up because of the delay in moving from Wallkill. Other things, such as life-support systems, had priority. A lot of craftspeople ended up exhibiting on the campgrounds. There were some booths with leatherworkers, ceramists, jewelers, and painters, but the craft area wasn't well prepared. There was a camp near the Hog Farm called Movement City, where emissaries from the radical movements bivouacked. It served as a communications center. Movement City held Abbie Hoffman's entourage, the Weathermen, the Students for a Democratic Society, the Movement for a Democratic Society, and other smaller groups. They intended to put out a newsletter every day to inform the crowd what was going on at the festival, and they did install a line of phone booths, the only ones available. The Movement City group thought that people would come by as they did at college campus gigs to pick up political literature, but they were mistaken. Collectively located (next to the Hog Farm), they could not infiltrate the crowd, and the good friendly vibrations successfully prevented them from taking a strong political stance. The Movement people say the Movement failed at Woodstock, but in reality it was a positive experience in that they lived together peacefully for one moment with the hip culture. That suited Michael Lang and his group because the celebration they envisioned had nothing to do with the far Left or far Right.

Joel, John, Michael, and Artie had had to deal with Abbie Hoffman before the festival. They thought his group might disrupt the festival with riots, put acid in drinking water, or demand microphone time. Abbie was getting a lot of pressure from radical Left groups at that time about having a real youth (not just college youth) following. He wanted to prove that he could make waves with the kids, so he put pressure on the promoters who met with him. It turned out that Abbie's group wanted money, which was a relief to the promoters, who finally bought off the underground with several thousand dollars. They were to "help" at the festival, to come and see that the people were going to get what they should, and protect them from a "capitalist ripoff," which was Hoffman's charge at the time. Abbie agreed not to speak at the festival. He did anyway, when crazed after working 22 straight hours in the hospital tent. He ran onto the stage, grabbed the microphone, and yelled "Free John Sinclair!" Abbie's point was that as long as John Sinclair was in jail for possession of just two joints, the festival was a contradiction.

In any case, the booths set up for Movement City were barely used. The printing press arrived late and was ruined by the mud. And many of the radicals, with a keen sense of what was happening, were caught up themselves in the prevailing party and diverted from politics.

By Thursday a lot of the audience had arrived. They were in the field by the thousands. The ticket booths were not up yet, nor the hurricane fence projected to deter gatecrashers. Friday morning the promoters made the announcement that it was a free festival. Not that they had planned it so; they were compelled by the circumstances they found themselves in. There was no system to collect

115

the money and no means to isolate the paying from the would-be freebees. There was a small controversy about why some people had to pay and others didn't. But even though thousands had paid for tickets at the shops and by mail order, the fact that most were admitted free added ultimately to the flavor of the festival.

On Thursday, 346 off-duty New York City policemen hired as "ushers" walked off their jobs at the site. The reason was given in the August 15 *New York Times*:

AGE OF AQUARIUS DAWNS MINUS COPS
Police Commissioner Howard R. Leary sent a special notice to all city precincts. In it he reminded those men "engaged to do various work assignments" during the three-day festival that their employment would violate the 1967 moonlighting regulations, which forbid policemen to have outside jobs involving security work.

On Friday morning the threat of being overwhelmed with fans caused the promoters to issue a news release to the radio stations asking all music fans on the road to the festival to turn back. Three helicopters were used to guide traffic and break up roadblocks. There was a traffic jam spreading 15 miles around the town of Bethel, a full four hours before the music was scheduled to start on Friday. People were

hiking three to 12 miles to get to the site. Cars were being abandoned for 15 miles along Route 17B and on every other road leading to the site. Headlines around the country read: TRAFFIC UPTIGHT AT HIPPIE FEST and JAM SESSION ON WAY TO FEST and THE GREAT ROCK-PILE UP. A liquor store as far away as Stone Ridge, 60 miles from the festival, had sold out of wine by Friday night! The owner will never forget it. "They were so frightening, but they were polite and they didn't steal one bottle."

Fragments of the counterculture were coming from as far away as Seattle and Tucson, all heading for the promised land. No one was coming to pay homage to a particular person or idol, nor were they coming for a political convention or rally, or a particular religious meeting, or a spectator sport such as a football game. In a sense they were coming for all these things and more, the loosest and freest combination of motives imaginable; but music was at the center.

"Pilgrims" on the roads remember the emotional surge they felt when it was really evident that this was not only the most colossal traffic jam they had even been in, but it was the coming together of a new consciousness composed of their own age group. There were Hondas and two-wheelers, vans, trucks, and friendly people sitting on fenders and hoods and lounging in open trunks. If they didn't try passing to the left through alfalfa fields, ending up in a mudhole, they were stuck in the long, endless line of vehicles; they were meeting people, toking on joints, and passing bottles of wine up and down the highways. They got caught up in perhaps the most frantic excitement of their lives before they even got to the site.

The townspeople were friendly. The Amish in their black hats down the way from the festival sat on their porches behind the white picket fences gazing at all the thousands of young people. The kids waved the sign V for peace and were happy. They didn't bother anyone. Some set up campsites all along the back roads.

Meanwhile, attorneys for the nearby Monticello Raceway were at work preparing a suit against Woodstock Ventures for blocking the public roads. By Saturday the New York Port Authority stopped selling bus tickets for destinations to any point remotely near the festival site. At the Canadian border, drivers were told to turn back, and New York State troopers closed off the thruway exits at the Big Apple Rest and Harriman. Travelers were forced to drive farther north, where they had to search out back roads to the site. It was estimated that there were another 500,000 en route to the festival who couldn't get there.

For the natives, all those caravans of strange vehicles and even stranger-looking young Americans composed probably the most fantastic, colorful parade they had ever witnessed. It was probably the largest spontaneous parade in history.

The kaleidoscopic clothing the crowds wore was the antithesis of the Paris and New York fashion worlds. Clothing was created out of their lifestyle: the new patriotism, the urge to be fresh and flamboyant. It was a time when people made a social-political statement by the kind of clothing they wore. They could turn other people around with clothing and long hair. Dressing with the same flair and freedom is less startling today, but back then it was a mark of defiance to wear frontier-influenced, deerskin-fringed jackets, cowboy shirts and boots, especially combined with long hair. It was an insult to solid red-blooded Americans, a defiant infringement on their territory. Granny glasses and long, pioneer, down-home dresses reflected the communal lifestyle. The conventions of patriotic dress were challenged: the Stars and Stripes were transmogrified into shorts, hats, boots, belts, and headbands. This was a new wave of patriotism, which to the rest of America

Tom Law

117

seemed un-American. Middle America could never equate long hair with patriotism, even though it was a style of the pioneers. After the festival, by 1970, the use of the American flag as clothing was generally outlawed, but the new spirit influenced fashions throughout the affluent world almost immediately.

Loose-fitting white shirts and pants, guru gowns, exotic, full, tie-dyed silk dresses and shirts, batik imports, and saris exemplified India's influence in the Sixties culture. There was plenty of army surplus, showing the practical value of recycled clothing. The era's psychedelic taste was integrated with everything; clothing, guitars, tents, and bags were painted in Day-Glo, Art Nouveau, and futuristic designs consistent with the period's style. Vans and buses were painted too. Displaying peace symbols and decals of flowers were acts and signs of identification with the peace movement or drug movement or both. They could get your car stopped and searched anywhere and anytime. Remember, this was the period when the "other" world out there was still wrapped up in the conviction that the Vietnam war was the patriotic "right way"; and it was the time when these so-called hippies threatened the straight world with drugs, sex, and "free" dress.

Being stoned was part of it, but at the festival stoned meant being up, not down. There was a lot of pot, hash, and pills, mostly LSD. The festival took place for the active force in the hip culture, so the passive, introverted, hard-drug users didn't even want to be a part of this extroverted event. Drugs were, to many of that era, a means to enlightenment. They were considered valid means to new states of awareness and religious experiences. This high feeling radiated throughout the festival.

A lot of people were on acid, but even those who weren't could "feel" the highness. Certainly Michael Lang felt grass had a better effect on people than alcohol, which could bring out their hostile, volatile side. He took great pleasure in discouraging the sale of alcohol, the "drug" of the Establishment, which discouraged the sale of grass.

The local and state police had been given the word to go easy on drug arrests. The pot smokers realized they had protection in numbers, and the police took little notice of them. Nor were the natives yelling, "Are you a boy or a girl?" The hippies were being left alone. One

state police sergeant said, "As far as I know, the narcotics guys are not arresting anybody for grass. If they did, there isn't enough space in Sullivan or the next three counties to put them in." But police enlightenment hadn't spread far enough. Farther away from the site a few cars were spot-checked, and most of the arrests over those three days were made on the less congested highways. Thirty arrests were reported at the Canadian border 500 miles away. Only in or near White Lake was there safety in being with your own kind, particularly when there were 500,000 of them!

There was a tremendous number of people who were there and didn't know really what to expect. They were newcomers, innocents, so to speak, without an idea of what the festival was going to be. Clean-cut college kids, people from the straight life who just brought their

thermos jugs and picnic baskets. But all of a sudden they were *part of it:* the group experience, the vibes, the music. Even the musicians, who'd been around and around, said it was the *crowd* that was the mind-blower. It was the crowd that became the most important element for everyone. No one could have imagined what it would be like to be in a crowd of 500,000 people, because there may never have been as large a peaceful gathering in the history of the world!

There were lots of kids, too, whose hair was just beginning to grow long and who were in pure awe of the Hog Farmers. They had never seen the likes of these freaks, who were so benevolent but looked like a species of bikers. They saw beautiful banners with symbols of yin and yang, or with red dragons on four-leaf clovers displayed on the booths. There were street musicians playing flutes, congas, and mouth harps; there was dancing, performing dervishes on rugs, and street-theater groups. People shared whatever they brought. There was a sharing of the campsites, sleeping bags and tents, water, food, grass, and a sharing of the dawn, nighttime, and sunsets. Everybody shared the glory of rain and mud and the civic problems of the three-day city. Participation and sharing were the underlying themes, while overriding all was the feeling of happiness. Barriers were broken down. Everyone was swapping and buying and selling. A lot of money changed hands at first, but after Friday there was so much exchanging of everything that the private-property instinct was eclipsed. There was, of

course, lots of grass. People were rolling it up and handing it around. There were free kilos of grass brought in by people sympathetic to the cause.

Hordes of people were looking for and finding friends. The year 1969 was a time for bulletin boards as communication devices, and messages were left there or announced over the microphone or even left hanging from trees. Communes from all over and people from other special groups were at the festival: the Swamis, Motherfuckers, SDS, MDS, Peaceniks, the Hot Chow Mein, the Hara Krishnas, the Yippies, the Meher Babaites, the Intrepid Travelers, the Rainbow People, and the Merry Pranksters. The latter three came all the way from Oregon. Babbs, Ken Kesey's right-hand man, came with the Pranksters, but Kesey himself stayed behind. Many people set up their lifestyles by a tree or next to a stone wall. It was as if they were saying, "This is what we do in our commune, or in our apartment in New York City, or wherever." Individuals and groups wanted to show others their way of life. One person brought his lamb and walked around with it. He held a big sign which read, "Don't eat animals, love them."

Everyone remembers rain and mud, impressions of nudity at the lake, and campfires at night. It rained on and off Thursday through Sunday. The loudspeakers of the U.S. Committee to Aid the National Liberation Front were announcing, "Get your dry Che Guevara T-shirts." Some people took off their clothes and just danced naked in the rain. There were mass run-and-slide-in-the-mud gambols. People were feeling so good that most of them

will tell you today that they were immunized to physical discomfort. Headlines, however, read: MIRED IN A SEA OF MUD.

The Hog Farm attitude of work-and-joke in the face of disaster made it possible for people to get through all the hardships—the rain and mud, the bad trips, and the food shortage. The emergencies that happened were handled by a crowd that was already turned on to the fact that the ultimate responsibility was theirs. The Hog Farm's concept made the individual a star; the audience was the performer to watch: a collection of stars that made one big entity.

Early Friday night each person in the crowd was asked to light a match, and there were matches as far as one could see. It was not just an evening's concert; it was days and nights of music. It lasted while people were in front of the stage. It lasted while they were in the lake swimming. It lasted every place they went.

People began to feel a new kind of relationship. You didn't have to know a person to give her or him a hug and get a hug back. They were experiencing a submersion into a common consciousness, but it was too big for serious philosophizing then. It was enough just to take it in. Hara Krishnas compared the crowd to the multitudes in India who flock to the banks of the Ganges to bathe in the sacred waters in an ancient ritual. Some people say it was like a huge religious event. Steven

HENRY DILTZ

Stills said it was like a combination of the Macedonian Army and the Twelve Tribes of Israel. Michael Young was so impressed by the rolling hills beyond, covered with tents and campfires at night, that they reminded him of the Battle of Agincourt in *Henry V*. There was a feeling of immersion into a vastness of humanity, of what seemed to some the beginnings of a new age.

Whatever one thought about the festival, it was certainly awesome and exciting, a new overnight city, a living space where all important needs were being taken care of. Nobody hassled you, and you did what you wanted, even though there wasn't much you wanted to do. It was enough just sitting on the grass, feeling and listening. You could just be.

There was no crowding—not like Altamont, where people wanted to crowd into the only space near the stage, which seemed like the center of the earth. Woodstock's sound stage was big enough; in fact, it was the biggest in the country: 60 feet wide and 70 feet deep—bigger than the one in New York's Metropolitan Opera House— so people could see the whole natural amphitheater and still feel fairly close to it. Not only were there so many other places for people to go, but the Hog Farm had its own stage with entertainment always going on: a lot of vaudeville—and some of the stars booked by the festival even went over and performed there.

The stars and musicians booked were in some ways a bit better off than the crowd. They were flown in by helicopter from where they stayed at the Holiday Inn and

LEE MARSHALL

flown out again. Some, like The Band, were flown from Woodstock direct to the festival site. The performers were favored with all the food they wanted (Potbelly's Restaurant was there just for them), and they could sit down and have lots of space. But they, too, were part of the rain and the mud and the huge crowd, all experiencing the same vibes. Many of the stars who played there have said it was their peak experience.

The freak-out tent (first-aid station) was between the stage and the Hog Farm. People on a bad trip, or overwhelmed by too much input—people who couldn't handle it—found help and calm there. Frightened by the noise or the music, they could easily panic. Everyone would help other people not able to cope and would bring them to the freak-out tent. There were also a lot of people wandering around in the crowd at the festival who had handled freak-outs before—veterans from places like Haight-Ashbury in San Francisco or the East Village in New York City—and they could take on anything that came along.

It is said that Dr. Abruzzie was so calm and confident that everyone around him was amazed, and the people who worked with him had that same kind of radiating confidence, even the many volunteers. Dr. Abruzzie reported that there were *no injuries as a result of violence.* There were injuries from people falling off cars and motorcycles, and working injuries like broken toes and fingers. There were stomach sicknesses, flus, and several hundred infections aggravated by the haphazard sanitary conditions, as well as poison ivy, heat prostration, and hepatitis. There was one death: a 17-year-old boy who fell asleep under some heavy equipment and no one saw him when they began to move the equipment out the next day. There was also one birth!

All the while, newspapers were sending out alarming reports. One paper said: "Young people die of dope. Young people experience reduction to stark animal status." Another reporter quoted alleged eyewitnesses; he wrote that they saw "young people writhing on the ground from drug overdoses," and "the smell in the air over the festival was like 'Egyptian filth.'" But the truth was people were doing their best, taking care of whatever problems occurred. A hospital was set up at the Rutherford School in Monticello, and people were taken out by helicopter to the hospital in Middletown. Helicopters flew in more doctors and supplies. They even ended up with more helicopters than were needed.

Hugh Romney (Wavy Gravy), the Hog Farm leader, talked people through their bad trips. He talked to the crowd from the stage about the "bad acid" that was there. When it appeared there was a food shortage, Wavy talked about it, making people laugh and telling them to come to the Hog Farm for rice. Helicopters flew in tons of extra grain, and the Sullivan County people responded to the emergency in all kinds of ways. Reportedly, they made 15,000 free breakfasts. They donated milk and sandwiches and set up a soup kitchen in Monticello. The stores sold out; St. Peter's Roman Catholic Church served food and about 100 slept there. A group back in Woodstock stayed up until 3:00 A.M. making peanut butter and jelly sandwiches and filling the Blues Magoos' drummer's truck full of the sandwiches and Cokes. When there was word out that the residents of White Lake were selling water to the kids, Max Yasgur was appalled. He put up a big sign—"Free Water"—on his barn; he became converted to the Woodstock Nation, to all those who were there or who were there in spirit. He called a press conference on his lawn and gave a 28-page testimonial to the festival.

Some of the local farmers were upset by the festival. One complained, "My property has been destroyed, thanks to Max Yasgur." Others besides Max came to grips with the people there. Ben Filipino, who owned land, called the festival "the seventh wonder of the world."

Late Saturday night was the peak of the festival. People started to leave Sunday morning, even before the late-afternoon thunderstorm, when the big migration home began. It had been tiring, excitement at a maximum and sleep at a minimum. Thousands had been there since Thursday. People were elated but exhausted. Less than one quarter of the vast crowd stayed on to hear Jimi Hendrix, who had requested to play last. It was the final highlight, and his interpretation of the national

anthem seemed the symbolic zenith of the festival. Newspaper headlines continued to inform the world what was happening: THE GREAT EXODUS . . . SOGGY RETREAT ENDS PLAGUED ROCK FAIR . . . THE DRIPPIES RETURN: SHOW PLENTY OF ZIP.

The Hog Farmers stayed on a week to clean up, as did literally thousands of others. It got windy and cold just before they finished, but the big job got done very fast, with flair and fun. A long plastic tube with "Peace" written on it was stuffed with napkins and other soft materials, and inflated with hydrogen. It took off through the air like a big snake until it was out of sight. Garbage was collected and then shaped to form the word "Peace," which could be seen in its entirety only from the air. One person started designing with bottles as they came in. It was creative-play garbage! The festival mood of joy and playfulness prevailed to the end.

The rest of the world didn't quite know what had happened at Woodstock. The newspapers reported people stranded, the shocking nudity, the drugs, the food shortage, and starvation. Some exaggerated the births as well as the deaths. Outside the festival one read: THE BENIGN MONSTER—ROCK RUMBLE IN RIP VAN WINKLE COUNTRY . . . BETHEL FARMERS CALL FAIR PLOT TO "AVOID THE LAW." The papers also carried positive words, quoting Max Yasgur: "What happened at Bethel this past weekend was that these young people together with our local residents turned the Aquarian Festival into a dramatic victory for the spirit of peace, good will, and human kindness." The *New York Post* quoted Lou Yank, head of Monticello police, who called the young people "the most courteous, considerate group of kids" he had ever dealt with. As late as August 18 (Monday morning) a *New York Times* article reflected a condescending, self-righteous attitude: "What kind of culture is it that can produce so colossal a mess? One youth dead and at least three others in hospitals from overdoses of drugs; and another dead from a mishap while sleeping in an open field"; and "The sponsors of this event, who apparently had not the slightest concern for the turmoil it would cause, should be made to account for their mismanagement. To try and cram several hundred thousand people into a 600-acre farm with only a few hastily installed sanitary facilities shows a complete lack of responsibility"; and "Last, but by no means least, was the fact that the great bulk of the freakish-looking intruders behaved astonishingly well, considering the disappointments and discomforts they encountered. They showed that there is real good under their fantastic exteriors, if it can just be aroused to some better purpose than the pursuit of LSD."

The world had to wait for those people who were at the festival to return to the backwoods and to the streets before they found out what a positive experience it had been for most of them. The hard core were so much into the festival, they didn't want to leave! They talked about staying and inventing a new way of life. They would put up windmills for energy, take care of Max's cows for him, and call the land "Jerusalem City."

—Jean Young